# Quick Guide

# BASEMENTS

# CREATIVE
## HOMEOWNER®

Manufactured in the United States of America

Editorial Director: Timothy O. Bakke
Art Director: Annie Jeon

Author: Mark Feirer
Editor: David Schiff
Assistant Editor: Patrick Quinn
Copy Editor: Kim Catanzarite
Graphic Designer: Michelle D. Halko
Illustrators: Ray Skibinski, Paul M. Schumm

Cover Design: Warren Ramezzana
Cover Illustrations: Paul M. Schumm

Current Printing (last digit)
10 9 8 7

Quick Guide: Basements
Library of Congress Catalog Card Number: 94-69656
ISBN: 1-880029-44-8 (paper)

CREATIVE HOMEOWNER®
A Division of Federal Marketing Corp.
24 Park Way
Upper Saddle River, NJ 07458
Web site: **www.creativehomeowner.com**

# C O N T E N T S

# S A F E T Y   F I R S T

Though all the designs and methods in this book have been reviewed for safety, it is not possible to overstate the importance of using the safest construction methods possible. What follows are reminders; some do's and don'ts of basic carpentry. They are not substitutes for your own common sense.

■ *Always* use caution, care, and good judgment when following the procedures described in this book.

■ *Always* be sure that the electrical setup is safe; be sure that no circuit is overloaded and that all power tools and electrical outlets are properly grounded. Do not use power tools in wet locations.

■ *Always* read container labels on paints, solvents, and other products; provide ventilation, and observe all other warnings.

■ *Always* read the manufacturer's instructions for using a tool, especially the warnings.

■ *Always* use hold-downs and push sticks whenever possible when working on a table saw. Avoid working short pieces if you can.

■ *Always* remove the key from any drill chuck (portable or press) before starting the drill.

■ *Always* pay deliberate attention to how a tool works so that you can avoid being injured.

■ *Always* know the limitations of your tools. Do not try to force them to do what they were not designed to do.

■ *Always* make sure that any adjustment is locked before proceeding. For example, always check the rip fence on a table saw or the bevel adjustment on a portable saw before starting to work.

■ *Always* clamp small pieces firmly to a bench or other work surface when using a power tool on them.

■ *Always* wear the appropriate rubber or work gloves when handling chemicals, moving or stacking lumber, or doing heavy construction.

■ *Always* wear a disposable face mask when you create dust by sawing or sanding. Use a special filtering respirator when working with toxic substances and solvents.

■ *Always* wear eye protection, especially when using power tools or striking metal on metal or concrete; a chip can fly off, for example, when chiseling concrete.

■ *Always* be aware that there is seldom enough time for your body's reflexes to save you from injury from a power tool in a dangerous situation; everything happens too fast. Be *alert!*

■ *Always* keep your hands away from the business ends of blades, cutters, and bits.

■ *Always* hold a circular saw firmly, usually with both hands so that you know where they are.

■ *Always* use a drill with an auxiliary handle to control the torque when large-size bits are used.

■ *Always* check your local building codes when planning new construction. The codes are intended to protect public safety and should be observed to the letter.

■ *Never* work with power tools when you are tired or under the influence of alcohol or drugs.

■ *Never* cut tiny pieces of wood or pipe using a power saw. Cut small pieces off larger pieces.

■ *Never* change a saw blade or a drill or router bit unless the power cord is unplugged. Do not depend on the switch being off; you might accidentally hit it.

■ *Never* work in insufficient lighting.

■ *Never* work while wearing loose clothing, hanging hair, open cuffs, or jewelry.

■ *Never* work with dull tools. Have them sharpened, or learn how to sharpen them yourself.

■ *Never* use a power tool on a workpiece—large or small—that is not firmly supported.

■ *Never* saw a workpiece that spans a large distance between horses without close support on each side of the cut; the piece can bend, closing on and jamming the blade, causing saw kickback.

■ *Never* support a workpiece from underneath with your leg or other part of your body when sawing.

■ *Never* carry sharp or pointed tools, such as utility knives, awls, or chisels, in your pocket. If you want to carry such tools, use a special-purpose tool belt with leather pockets and holders.

# PLANNING & DESIGN

Most basements are gloomy, so turning yours into a bright, cheery place can be challenging. The solution calls for efficient use of space, thoughtful lighting, and attention to color details. After that, you can concentrate on storage, furnishings, and fixtures that put the new spaces to work.

# Planning Rooms

According to building codes, all habitable rooms must have at least 70 square feet of area with not less than 84 inches in each horizontal direction. This standard is met easily, so from a practical standpoint, the size of most rooms is governed primarily by the size of the furnishings to be used. After all, a 70-square-foot bedroom is hardly a suitable location for a double bed. Keep in mind that the lack of abundant natural light in a basement can make rooms seem more cramped than they might seem elsewhere, so do not assume that the comfortable small room upstairs will feel the same if replicated downstairs.

Building codes also require that a basement room have a minimum ceiling height of 90 inches over at least one half of the room. The only exceptions are bathrooms, kitchens and hallways, which can have a ceiling height of 84 inches. If a quick measurement between the basement floor and the underside of the joists does not show at least that much headroom, it probably is not possible to obtain a permit to do the work.

Be sure to run phone wiring into the basement so it is not necessary to sprint up a flight of stairs every time the phone rings. Wiring is installed easily so plan to include modular jacks in several locations, particularly if the basement space is large.

## Planning a Bathroom

A bathroom can be small and yet serviceable at the same time. According to building codes the headroom in a bathroom can be as low as 84 inches. (That is 6 inches lower than the standard for other rooms.) In most cases, the location of the bathroom is determined by the accessibility of plumbing (drain, waste, and vent stacks) and ventilation (an outside window or mechanical ventilation). The plumbing is easier to install and less expensive if it can be tied into existing drain and vent pipes. Usually it is the addition of a toilet that most complicates a basement bathroom

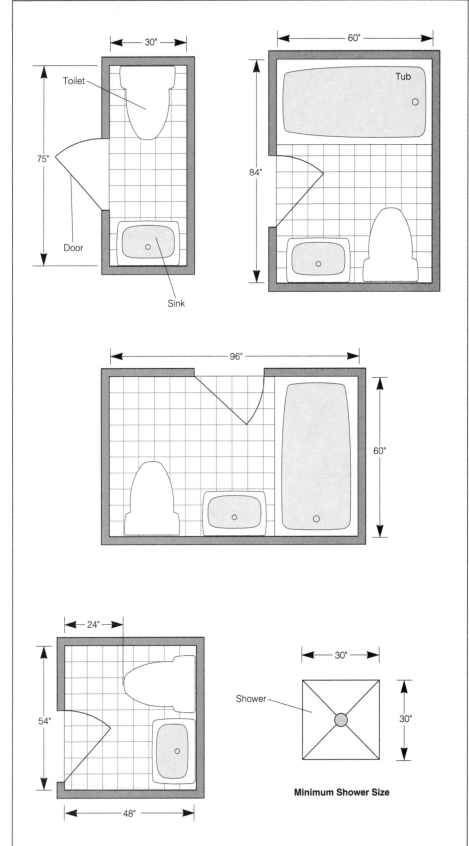

***Planning a Bathroom.*** The general space requirements for a bathroom are shown here. Headroom can be as low as 7 ft.

because it requires a bigger drain line than a sink or shower. Many people find that a basement shower, in addition to a sink and a toilet, is a considerable convenience, particularly if the basement contains a bedroom or two.

## Planning a Bedroom

The most important factor (and sometimes the most difficult) in bedroom planning is the provision of an emergency exit. The code requires that every bedroom, including those in the basement, must have direct access to a door or a window that can be used in an emergency. The window must meet certain requirements and the door must lead directly outdoors; it cannot lead to a bulkhead door. (See pages 46 to 52.)

**Closets.** The design and size of the closets in the bedroom depends in part on who is to use the room. A

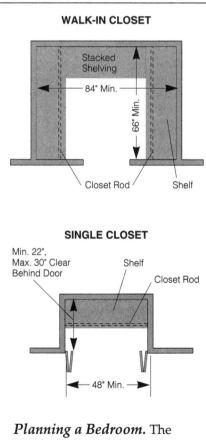

*Planning a Bedroom.* The standard sizes of closets are shown here.

modestly sized closet probably suffices in a guest bedroom, but a master bedroom calls for a bigger one. Manufacturers of closet shelving and storage systems are good sources for closet-design information and can show how to pack the most storage into the least amount of space.

## Planning a Recreation Room

The key to a great recreation room is versatility. Plan the space so that it can be used for a variety of activities. Wheeled storage cabinets, for example, can be rolled out of the way when hordes of 5-year-olds descend for a birthday party. Look for furniture that can be moved easily, build adaptable storage units, and install wall and floor surfaces that can stand up to the hard use this room typically sustains. Vinyl flooring, for example, is not stained by food spills (area rugs can give it "warmth") and wood paneling is more likely than drywall to survive chance encounters with cue sticks. An intense color or pattern can be overwhelming if used on all of the walls, but a spot of it (one brightly painted wall, for example) or some diagonal paneling can do wonders for a room. Wood paneling is a popular surface for recreation room walls because of its durability and visual warmth. In addition, the vertical lines of paneling create the illusion that the walls are taller than they are in reality.

There are no particular electrical requirements for the average recreation room, but again, the best plan is a versatile one. Make sure there are plenty of receptacles for appliances like vacuums. Extra cable outlets provide the opportunity to place a TV in various locations and several phone jacks can be surprisingly convenient. Look closely at your family's interests and plan for anything that might involve electricity, including lighted shelves for collectibles or outlets for fitness gear.

## Planning a Shop

The solid floor and sturdy walls of a basement lend themselves nicely to

the wear and tear that is typical of a wood shop. Since the height of the room is limited, however, additional horizontal space may be necessary to maneuver materials back and forth. Provide plenty of electrical outlets—they should be on a dedicated 20-amp circuit. Depending on the type of equipment used in the shop, 220v outlets as well as 110v outlets may be necessary. Given the proximity of the furnace and other combustion appliances (such as the water heater), and the lack of ventilation, it is not a good idea to work with stains and other wood finishing products in the confines of a basement shop.

**Shop Lighting.** Proper lighting is critical in a shop, so do not skimp on it. The ideal combination employs fluorescent lights for general lighting and incandescent lights for task and supplemental lighting. Wire the incandescents to one wall switch (because they hold up to being turned on and off frequently), and wire fluorescents to a second switch (to flip on only when you plan to be in the shop for a while). Fluorescent fixtures hung from short lengths of lightweight chain can be moved easily. Also, look for special break-resistant fluorescent and incandescent bulbs.

**Dust Control.** Keeping sawdust contained is another important precaution. Not only can dust be a nuisance when it ends up in living areas (or your lungs), but it also can play havoc with mechanical equipment. Furnaces call for special care. Dust quickly clogs the filters of a forced hot-air furnace, and even a boiler can be affected adversely by excessive dust. More importantly, however, excessive dust found near combustion appliances poses a fire hazard and under the right circumstances can even cause an explosion. (Keep a fire extinguisher handy.)

The best dust-control strategy is to use partition walls to isolate the shop from adjacent rooms. (See page 37.) To keep dust where it belongs, treat

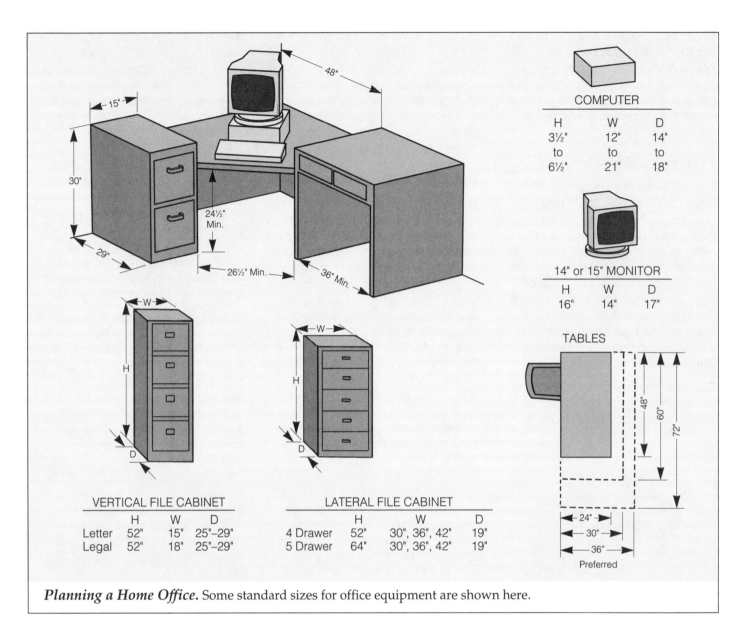

| COMPUTER | | |
|---|---|---|
| H | W | D |
| 3½" | 12" | 14" |
| to | to | to |
| 6½" | 21" | 18" |

| 14" or 15" MONITOR | | |
|---|---|---|
| H | W | D |
| 16" | 14" | 17" |

| VERTICAL FILE CABINET | | | |
|---|---|---|---|
| | H | W | D |
| Letter | 52" | 15" | 25"–29" |
| Legal | 52" | 18" | 25"–29" |

| LATERAL FILE CABINET | | | |
|---|---|---|---|
| | H | W | D |
| 4 Drawer | 52" | 30", 36", 42" | 19" |
| 5 Drawer | 64" | 30", 36", 42" | 19" |

TABLES

*Planning a Home Office.* Some standard sizes for office equipment are shown here.

each door that enters the shop as if it were an exterior door and weather-strip it accordingly. A portable dust collection system connected to each machine cuts down the dust considerably, though it does not eliminate dust altogether. At the very least, connect a shop vacuum to each source of sawdust as the work is done.

## Planning a Home Office

A home office is likely to be filled with electronic equipment including computers, printers, photocopiers, and fax machines. Allow plenty of outlets and, as a precaution, divide them into at least two separate circuits, if possible. Some pieces of home office equipment (such as a

laser printer) have significant power requirements, and if a circuit breaker trips while the computer is being used, important data may be lost.

Give particular thought to whether or not more than one phone line is necessary for your home office. It is possible for a computer modem and a telephone to "share" one line, but if the computer is used often for on-line research, it may be more convenient to put it on a second line. One reason to have two lines: If one line is an extension of your home number and the other is for business only, personal calls can be answered without leaving the office and business call expenses can be tracked separately.

Though it depends on the type of work you do, most offices require bookshelves as well as storage for files, office supplies and the like. Make every square foot count. For example, if a tall four-drawer file cabinet seems too awkward for the room consider using a pair of two-drawer units topped by a piece of plywood. By doing so, the file space is created as well as a stand for a printer or fax machine.

## Lighting

Lodged beneath an existing floor system and kept from daylight by tons of earth, most basements present a challenge for lighting design. Unlike

Not many people install chandeliers in their basements, but most other fixtures can be used. Pay attention to headroom when choosing ceiling fixtures. Also, different fixtures distribute light in different ways: Some illuminate a broad area whereas others spotlight small areas. Be sure to choose the fixture best suited to your needs.

**Incandescent Table Lamp.** These lamps are plugged into an outlet and can be controlled by a wall switch. They confine light to a relatively limited area.

**Wall Lights.** Wall lights provide focused illumination and, unlike track lighting, they do not compromise headroom.

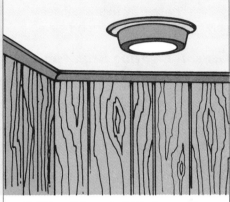

**Ceiling-Mounted Fixtures.** To maintain headroom choose one that is relatively flat.

**Fluorescent Tubes.** These lights, which are mounted behind a wood valence, spread light over an entire wall.

**Fluorescent Fixtures.** It is easy to fit fluorescent fixtures into a suspended ceiling system.

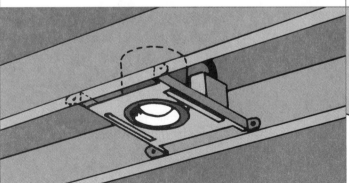

**Can-Type Lights.** These lights are recessed into joist cavities to provide unobtrusive spot or floor lighting.

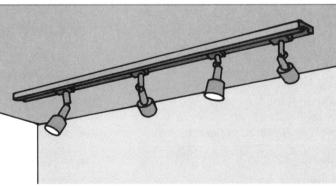

**Track Lighting.** This type of lighting can be fitted with floodlights for general illumination or with spotlights for accent lighting.

above-grade rooms, a basement cannot easily be brightened with the addition of a window or skylight. In many cases the only windows to work with are those mounted high in the wall. Another complication relates to the proportions of the space. With so much floor area beneath relatively low ceilings, basement rooms can feel confining and uncomfortably cavelike.

## *General Lighting Requirements*

To provide a suitable amount of natural light, building codes generally require that all habitable rooms have an amount of glazing (window glass area) equal to 8 percent or more of the floor area (for exceptions, see below). As far as the provision of daylight goes, it does not matter if the glazing is fixed or operable. For rooms located partially below grade, this amount is difficult to achieve, so for them the code allows an exception to the requirement for natural lighting.

**Types of Bulbs.** Natural lighting can be entirely forgone if artificial light, capable of producing an average of 6 lumens per square foot over the area of the room, is provided.

Lumens are a measure of the total amount of light emitted by a light bulb; the more lumens a bulb has, the more light it emits. Six lumens per square foot is not a difficult target to achieve. To get a handle on the type of lighting needed measure the width and length of a room, then use the chart on this page to see what type of bulb (and how many of them) are needed to meet code. Once the type of bulb has been chosen, it is easy to figure out the type of light fixture needed.

Note that the 6-lumen figure is for general lighting, and that it is an average required in each room. When the lighting for a room is planned, the provision of general lighting is the first priority. After that, task lighting and accent lighting can be added as needed. Special-purpose rooms, such as bathrooms and home offices, may have additional lighting

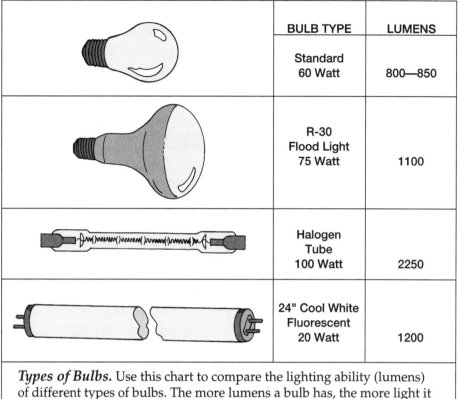

| BULB TYPE | LUMENS |
|---|---|
| Standard 60 Watt | 800—850 |
| R-30 Flood Light 75 Watt | 1100 |
| Halogen Tube 100 Watt | 2250 |
| 24" Cool White Fluorescent 20 Watt | 1200 |

*Types of Bulbs.* Use this chart to compare the lighting ability (lumens) of different types of bulbs. The more lumens a bulb has, the more light it emits. The wattages listed are common in residential lighting. Increasing the wattage increases a bulb's luminosity.

requirements (see pages 6 and 8).

Some parts of the country are prone to frequent, although short, power outages, particularly during the winter. Though not required by building codes, it is a good idea to plug an emergency light into one or two outlets in the basement. This small, inexpensive light is powered by a rechargeable battery that maintains a charge while plugged into an outlet. When power is lost the battery takes over, providing enough light for inhabitants to navigate through an otherwise dark room.

## *Designing with Light*

To maximize the effectiveness of lighting use light-colored surfaces wherever possible; doing so helps reflect light around the room. Dark paneling or carpeting, on the other hand, tends to "soak up" light. Use a variety of light sources (if possible) to provide maximum flexibility when it comes to setting a mood or producing extra light for activities. Some

types of lighting can be regulated by dimmer switches for a range of lighting levels.

**Light Quality.** Because a basement relies heavily on artificial light, the quality of that light is worth ample consideration. Even if the quantity of light is adequate, the quality of the light can make or break a room.

Many people describe lighting quality in terms of its "coolness" or "warmth" and think this characteristic depends solely on the type of light bulb (fluorescent bulbs are thought to be cool while incandescent bulbs are considered warm). Because people tend to prefer warm light, they have traditionally avoided fluorescent lighting in homes. Modern fluorescent bulbs, however, are available in a variety of "temperatures." Add this to their energy-efficiency and they become well worth considering. If warm light is preferable, look for fluorescent bulbs rated at less than 3000 K (the Kelvin scale is used to measure lighting temperature).

# SIZING UP THE PROJECT

Once you have an idea of how you want to remodel the basement, a bit of necessary detective work is well worth the time and effort. Uncovering and solving potential problems at the start means being faced with fewer surprises and less expense later.

# Surveying the Basement

Not every basement can be converted to living space, and not every one that can is worth the effort. If, for example, the basement is short on headroom, the solution (lowering the floor level) may involve more effort and expense than it is worth. Likewise, if water problems cannot be eliminated despite your best efforts, the basement cannot be turned into a comfortable and healthy living space. Spend some time getting to know the basement before jumping into a remodeling job.

## Types of Basement Walls

The kind of walls found in the basement, and the condition of the walls, has a lot to do with how easy or hard the basement is to remodel. Basement walls, of course, are the inside surfaces of the foundation. They can be made of concrete block, poured concrete, stone or pressure-treated wood. Though some are easier to work with than others, none of the foundation types automatically prevents you from remodeling the basement. It is easy, for example, to install drywall or paneling on the walls of a pressure-treated wood foundation (the procedure is the same used for installing it on wood-framed walls). On the other hand, a stone foundation sometimes has water problems that are difficult to remedy due to the irregular nature of the materials. Walls of concrete block or poured concrete are the most common.

**Concrete Block Walls.** A foundation that is made with concrete blocks is easy to identify because of the grid pattern that is created by horizontal and vertical mortar joints. Each block has a hollow core and the inside and outside faces of the block are connected by integral webs. The hollow structure of the block makes it lighter (and easier to work with) and allows the wall to be strengthened with the addition of reinforcing bar (called

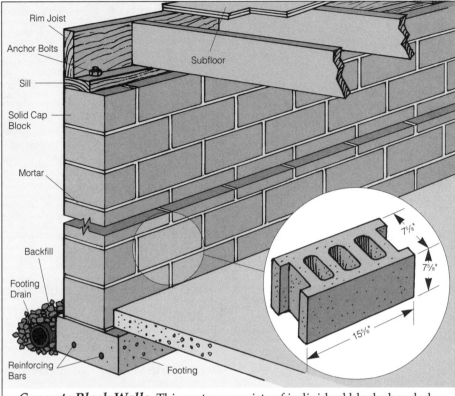

*Concrete Block Walls.* This system consists of individual blocks bonded together with mortar. The blocks shown here are those used most often for residential construction.

rebar) mortared into the cores. Most blocks are identified by their nominal dimension because that's the measurement used to calculate how many blocks are needed in a wall. Nominal 8x8x16-inch blocks typically used in residential construction actually measure  $7\frac{5}{8}$ x $7\frac{5}{8}$ x $15\frac{5}{8}$  inches. The extra 3/8 inch allows for the mortar joints.

Blocks (in the building trades they are called concrete masonry units or CMUs) are stacked one atop the other. Mortar placed between each row and each block bonds the units and results in a strong, solid wall. Because of this construction method, the ultimate strength and water-resistance of the basement wall depends not just on the condition of the blocks but on the condition of the mortar as well.

**Poured Concrete Walls.** A poured concrete wall is monolithic and has a smooth surface. To build such a wall, concrete (a mixture of sand, gravel, water and portland cement) is poured into metal or plywood form work. Steel

reinforcing bars often are placed in the forms prior to the pour. The bars strengthen a concrete wall and help resist cracking.

**Other Types of Walls.** In some areas of the country, particularly the Midwest, builders may frame a house on top of a foundation of 2x8 or larger studs and plates that have been pressure-treated with chemicals to resist decay. This is a relatively new type of foundation. Sheathed on the outside with pressure-treated plywood and detailed carefully to eliminate water infiltration, the foundation can be insulated and finished like a standard framed wall.

Stone foundations still can be found in areas of the country, such as the Northeast, where some houses predate the availability of concrete. Though the type of stone typically varies according to that which was available locally, the foundation usually was laid up with mortar. To

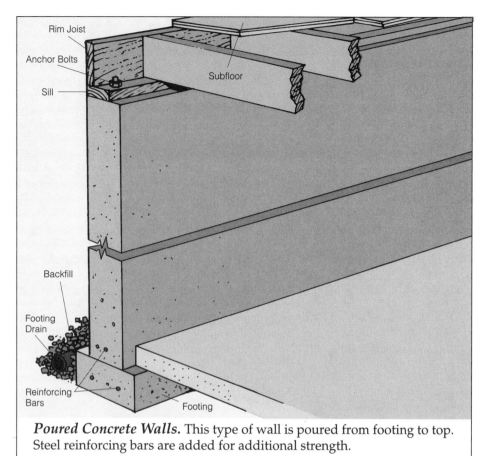

**Poured Concrete Walls.** This type of wall is poured from footing to top. Steel reinforcing bars are added for additional strength.

Labels: Rim Joist, Anchor Bolts, Sill, Subfloor, Backfill, Footing Drain, Reinforcing Bars, Footing

find out if the foundation is in good condition, it is well worth having a mason inspect it before remodeling the basement.

## Looking for Trouble

Before beginning work, there is more you must know about your basement. It is easier to deal with an insurmountable problem before a small mountain of building materials is delivered to the front yard rather than after.

**Foundation Cracks.** Figuring out what to do about foundation cracks is more art than science. Small hairline cracks in a concrete wall are sometimes the fault of improper curing. Larger cracks in a foundation wall usually are due to settling. Both types can be repaired with hydraulic cement if the crack is not an active one. (See page 21.) In other words, the crack is patched easily if whatever caused it in the first place is no longer a problem. If the foundation is in the process of settling,

however, or if some other factor is stressing the foundation, cracks that are patched today may open again tomorrow. Before the cracks can be fixed permanently, the problem has to be eliminated.

To determine if a crack is active, draw lines across it in several places. Then check for evidence of movement over the course of several seasons.

**Inadequate Headroom.** According to building codes, a room in the basement must have a minimum ceiling height of 90 inches over at least one half of the room. The only exceptions are bathrooms, kitchens, and hallways which are allowed a ceiling height of 84 inches. Minimum headroom measurements are taken from finished surfaces. If a measurement between the basement floor and the underside of the joists does not meet these standards, it may be impossible to get a permit.

**Poor Access.** Getting into the basement usually is not a problem. The stair might have to be repaired, but at least it already exists. When it comes to basement bedrooms, however, having an exit in case of an emergency also becomes an issue. According to code, all bedrooms in the basement must have a means of emergency exit. A door that leads directly outside from a bedroom (and not to a bulkhead door; see page 52) qualifies as an emergency exit. If no such door exists, there must be a window that can be used instead. The require-

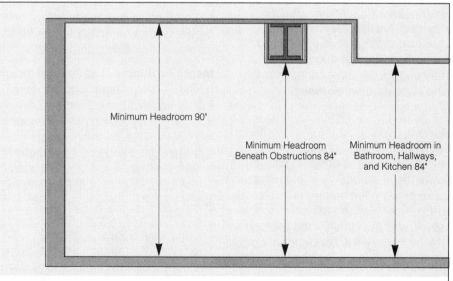

Minimum Headroom 90"

Minimum Headroom Beneath Obstructions 84"

Minimum Headroom in Bathroom, Hallways, and Kitchen 84"

**Inadequate Headroom.** Building codes allow less headroom in bathrooms, kitchens, and hallways than in other living areas.

ments for such a window (called an egress window) is 5 square feet of openable area. If remodeling plans include a bedroom make the egress issue the first order of business.

**Lack of Air Circulation.** All rooms become uncomfortably stuffy when the air in the room is not renewed with fresh air periodically. Building code calls for operable windows equal in size to at least 4 percent of the room's floor space. (Do not confuse this figure with the amount of glazing needed to provide natural daylight in a basement; see page 8.) In a basement, however, this is not an easy percentage to achieve, so the code offers the following exception:

If a room is served by an "approved" mechanical ventilation system that is capable of changing the air every 30 minutes, operable windows are not required. An "approval" must be given by your local code officials, however, so check with them before deciding to pursue this exemption.

**Moisture Problems.** Of all the possible roadblocks to making the basement livable, moisture problems can be the thorniest to solve. Water is incredibly persistent, and under the right circumstances can make its way through walls that are considered impermeable. Another source of moisture is the condensation that forms as warm, moist air reaches the cold surface of a masonry wall. Some moisture problems can be remedied (see page 20), but major problems may call for professional assistance and considerable expense.

An easy test for water problems is done by taping pieces of aluminum foil to various places on the walls and floor. Seal the edges tightly and leave the test patches in place for several days. If moisture droplets appear beneath the foil after several days, moisture is migrating through the masonry; if they appear on top of the foil, the problem is condensation.

When looking for water problems investigate the underside of the floor sheathing for signs of leaks. Now is

*Moisture Problems.* Tape a patch of aluminum foil to several sections of the floor and walls. If moisture droplets collect underneath or on top of the foil, a moisture problem exists and must be corrected.

the time to fix faulty pipes and fixtures. Inspect the sheathing and the sides of the joists for brownish stains which may indicate an active leak or an old leak that has since been repaired. If the stain is spongy when probed with a flat-blade screwdriver, an active leak exists somewhere.

**Insect Problems.** The floor system of most houses rests on wood "plates" that are bolted to the foundation. If the house has a problem with wood-destroying insects, this is where the evidence will be found. Check the outer foot or so of the floor joists, the inside surface of the rim joist and the wood frame of every basement window. Keep an eye out for signs of powder-post beetles, carpenter ants and nonsubterranean termites. Signs of insect problems include swarming insects, a series of pinholes in the wood and small, powdery piles of sawdust beneath affected wood. If

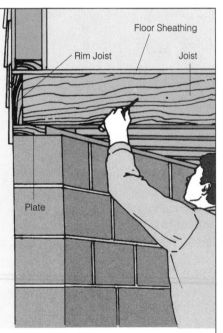

*Insect Problems.* Use an awl to investigate the rim joist area. Rotten or bug-infested wood yields easily.

*Sagging Joists.* Sight across the underside of the joists to spot those that are out of line. Then check to see if the whole floor system is sagging.

things look suspicious rap the wood with your knuckles—infested wood sounds different than solid wood. To search for rot or insect damage use the tip of a scratch awl to poke at the rim joist, the plate, the ends of the joists and window framing (even if it looks sound). Rotten or bug-infested wood yields easily. (Building inspectors have been known to use a ski pole with a sharpened tip to poke at the rim joists, eliminating the need for a ladder). Infested areas must be treated by a professional exterminator before remodeling work can begin.

**Sagging Joists.** Sight across the underside of the floor joists to better see if they are out of line. Those that are out of line probably are damaged but most likely can be repaired easily. If all the joists sag noticeably, however, it may be that they are improperly supported or undersized. In either case, a remedy is readily available. (See page 20.)

# Discovering Potential Health Hazards

## *Radon*

Radon is a colorless, odorless radioactive gas that comes from the natural breakdown of uranium in soil, rock, and water. When breathed into the body, molecules of radon lodge in the lungs and lead to an increased risk of lung cancer. The incidence of radon is not restricted to certain areas of the country. Radon typically moves up through the ground and into a house through cracks and holes in the foundation (though they are not the only source). Because it tends to concentrate in rooms closest to the ground, it is particularly important to test for radon before converting a basement to living space. If test results indicate that there is a problem, radon reduction techniques are relatively easy to incorporate into remodeling plans.

**Testing for Radon.** It is fairly easy to test a house for radon. Do not rely on tests performed on other houses in the area—even homes that are next door to each other can have different levels of the gas. There are two basic types of radon tests:

■ Active tests call for special equipment and generally are the most accurate, but require a specially trained technician.

■ Passive tests include a variety of inexpensive testing products available at hardware stores, home center stores, or by mail from state-certified testing laboratories. These devices are exposed to the air inside the basement for a specified length of time and then they are mailed to a testing laboratory. Long-term passive tests offer a good indication of the year-round average radon exposure but must be in place for at least 90 days. Short-term tests, though not as accurate, can be completed in as little as 48 hours. Short-term testing typically is done under closed-house conditions. That means keeping all windows and doors closed (except for normal entry and exit) and refraining from using fans or other machines that bring outside air into the house. The home's heating system may be operated normally while the test is being performed, but the cooling system can be used only if it does not draw outside air into the house. A short-term test indicates closely enough whether or not a major problem exists. However, if a short-term test indicates that there is a problem, it is recommended that another test be conducted to confirm the diagnosis.

If testing indicates a level of radon of more than 4 pico curies per liter (pc/c) of air (a standard measurement of radon), take steps to reduce the radon by employing a process called mitigation. A level of about 1.3 pc/l is considered average and generally not worth the expense of mitigation.

**Reducing Radon.** Sealing cracks and other openings in the foundation is a basic part of most radon-reduction approaches. However, the federal Environmental Protection Agency does not recommend sealing alone because it has not been proven effective. In most cases, reduction systems that incorporate pipes and fans to vent air to the outdoors are preferred. Contact a licensed mitigation specialist.

### Asbestos

Asbestos is a fibrous mineral found in rocks and soil throughout the world. Alone or in combination with other materials, asbestos was once fashioned into a variety of building materials because it is strong, durable, fire retardant and an efficient insulator. Unfortunately, it also is a carcinogen. Once inhaled, asbestos fibers lodge in the lungs. Because the material is so durable, it remains in the lung tissue and becomes concentrated as repeated exposure occurs over time. Asbestos can cause cancer of the lungs and stomach among those who have prolonged work-related exposure to it. Home health risks arise when age, accidental damage, normal cleaning,

or remodeling activities cause the asbestos-containing materials to crumble, flake, or deteriorate. The health effects of low exposures to asbestos are uncertain but experts cannot provide assurances that even a small level of exposure is completely safe.

According to the EPA, houses constructed in the United States during the last 20 years are less likely to contain asbestos products than houses built earlier. Asbestos sometimes is found around pipes and furnaces, in some vinyl flooring materials and ceiling tiles and in exterior roofing and some wallboards. It also is mixed with other materials and troweled or sprayed around pipes, ducts and beams.

***Caution:*** *If you suspect asbestos has been used in your basement, have the area inspected by a professional before remodeling. Never attempt to remove asbestos yourself. The materials must be removed and disposed of according to strict guidelines. This is a job for trained specialists only. You'll find these*

*experts in the Yellow Pages under Asbestos Removal and Abatement.*

## Planning for Utilities

### Heating System

As part of a preconstruction review of the basement, give some thought to how the space will be heated. Though it might seem as if the surrounding earth would be a pretty good insulator, it is not. In climates that require heat, making the basement comfortable in the winter almost always calls for supplemental heating. If the house is heated by one of the following systems, the system can be extended to the basement: forced-air heat (oil, gas, or electric), electric baseboard heat or hydronic (hot water) baseboard heat.

**Electric Heaters.** In many cases, an electric baseboard or fan-forced electric heater supplies all the heat necessary for a basement and can be added no matter what type of heating system already exists. The electric service panel, however, must be

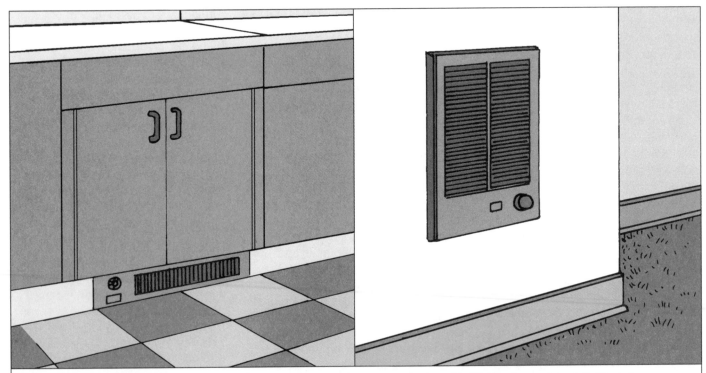

***Electric Heaters.*** If space is tight an electric kick-space heater can be installed beneath a cabinet (left). A fan-forced electric heater mounted in a wall can heat an entire room if sized properly (right).

able to accommodate the additional load. Contact a heating contractor for advice before applying for a building permit. He or she will be able to suggest a suitable heater size.

## Electrical System

Though it is possible to extend an existing electrical circuit into the basement, doing so may overload the circuit. In addition, extending a circuit that already exists does not provide enough power for most conversions. (Besides, since the electrical service panel usually is in the basement, it is easy to run new circuits.) If your electrical box does not have room for a new circuit, however, you might be able to tap into an existing circuit in the basement—just be sure not to overload it. Add two or more circuits for a home office or for an unusually large basement. While you are planning where to run wires, do not forget to plan for a phone line as well. Add an additional circuit to supply each permanently installed electric heater. Basement circuits must meet the same electrical code requirements that govern other living spaces in the house.

Service to the house must be at least 100 amperes to accommodate the extra electrical load. If your house has 200-ampere service, as most newer homes do, adding circuits is not a problem. Most homes built before 1941 have two-wire electric service which may limit the number and type of electrical appliances that can be used. Newer houses have three-wire service. Consult a licensed electrician to determine whether or not the present system can be added to, modified, or upgraded.

## Plumbing System

**Water Supply.** If your water comes from a well, the ability of the system to support a new bathroom is determined by the pump and the capacity of the well. A plumbing system that is supplied by municipal sources, however, usually can accommodate the addition of another bathroom.

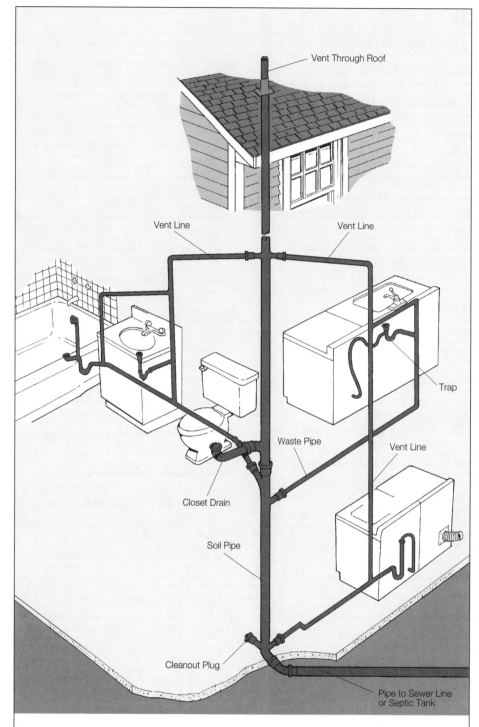

*Drainage and Venting.* The drain, waste, vent system transports waste from fixtures and appliances to the sewer or septic tank.

**Drainage and Venting.** Drainage of waste water and sewage is done through a network of pipes that transport them to the sewer or septic tank. In order for these pipes to drain freely they must be connected to a system of vent pipes that lead up to and through the roof. With some careful planning, new fixtures in a basement bathroom usually can tap into the existing system. Try to locate the new bathroom as closely as possible to existing drain lines.

# Who Will Do the Work?

Building codes usually allow a homeowner to work on or add to every part of his or her own house, including the plumbing and electrical systems. Depending on the magnitude of the project, however, you may want to turn part or all of the work over to a professional. And if you have to borrow money for the project, the lender may require certain parts of the job to be completed professionally. Call several lenders to determine their policies.

# Building Codes

Building regulations have been with us at least since the eighteenth century B.C., when the Code of Hammurabi mandated death to the son of any builder whose building collapsed and killed the son of its owner. (Hammurabi was a king of Babylonia whose code of laws, found on a column at Susa, is one of the greatest ancient codes.) Codes these days are not quite so severe, but they do have something in common with their predecessor in that they reflect the fundamental duty of government to protect the general health, safety, and welfare of its citizens.

Construction that takes place in the basement is covered by the same building codes that apply to work anywhere else in the house. The codes are published in book form. The book (or books) may be available at your local building

*Do You Need a Permit?*

Permits and inspections enforce the building codes. A permit essentially is a license that authorizes someone to do the work; an inspection verifies that the work has been done properly. Minor repairs and remodeling work usually do not call for a permit but if the job consists of extending the water supply and the drain, waste, vent system, or adding an electrical circuit, a permit may be necessary. A permit almost always is necessary when converting a basement to living space. Most states allow a homeowner to work on his or her own house (electrical and plumbing work included) if a permit is obtained first.

**Inspections.** Whenever a permit is required, it is necessary to schedule a time for a city or county building inspector to visit your home and examine the work. He or she makes sure that the work meets or exceeds the building codes. When obtaining a permit ask about the inspection schedule. For smaller projects an inspector might come out for a final inspection only, but for a larger project, several intermediate inspections may be necessary before a final inspection is done. In any case, it is your job to call for the inspection; not the inspector's job to figure out when you might be ready for one.

department. Those who do not want to purchase the books usually can find them in the reference section of the local library.

**Local Building Codes.** Not all of the United States is covered by the same building codes. In fact, each state, county, city, and town can use whatever codes best suit local building conditions. References to the building codes in this book correspond with the 1992 edition of the "One- and Two-Family Dwelling Code" published by The Council of American Building Officials (CABO). Though this is a widely recognized code, not all towns have adopted it, and those that have might use an earlier or later version. Before starting work check with local building

officials to determine the specific codes used in your area.

## Following Codes

Codes in your community might cover everything from the way your house is used to the materials you can use for building or remodeling it. In addition to building, electrical, and plumbing codes, your community also may have adopted some types of fire prevention codes, accessibility codes (requiring barrier-free access to buildings), or special construction codes (such as those requiring earthquake-resistance construction). Contact your local building department to determine the combination of codes that applies to your area.

# PREPARATION WORK

All major remodeling projects call for a significant amount of preparation before the tasks that really make a difference can be done. It is important to make sure the structure of the basement is sound and the space is free of moisture problems. If the big problems are solved first, the rest of the project will proceed smoothly.

# Repairing a Joist

It is likely that the joists in an old home have suffered damage over the years. Maybe a small crack turned into a large one, or perhaps someone cut into a joist for reasons that seemed reasonable at the time. Damaged joists, whatever their cause, must be repaired before a new ceiling is installed. Not all cracks compromise the strength of the joist but if the joist is sagging or if the crack runs clear to the bottom edge of the joist, repair is in order. Only in rare cases is it advised to remove a joist, even if it is seriously damaged. Remember, the floor sheathing is nailed into the floor joists, so pulling a joist risks damaging the finished floor above.

An existing joist can be reinforced and repaired by attaching an equal-sized joist alongside of it; this is called "sistering." The new lumber must be as long as the existing joist and of the same depth, and it is supported in the same locations. Maneuver the new joist into position (cutting off one corner of the joist may help), push the old joist back where it belongs, and then use 16d nails to nail the two together.

**Repairing a Joist.** A piece of lumber that is attached to the side of a joist to strengthen it is called a "sister." It must be almost the same length and exactly the same depth as the joist it supports. Cutting off the corner of opposite edges of the joist can help maneuver it into position.

# Eliminating Moisture Problems

A basement cannot be turned into a suitable living space unless it is guaranteed to stay dry. Water problems range in seriousness from mild condensation and seepage to periodic flooding. Given enough time and money, all water problems can be solved but that does not mean that the effort is justified.

## Determining the Source

Assuming that the plumbing does not leak, basement moisture comes either from seepage (water from outside the house leaking through walls or floor) or from condensation (the result of warm, moist air hitting a cold masonry wall or cold water pipes). The source of the water can be iden-

tified by performing a simple test (see page 14). If condensation is the problem, eliminate it either by installing a portable dehumidifier in the basement or by insulating the walls and water pipes.

Seepage water is more difficult to eliminate because it might be coming from any or all of the following sources:

**Gutter Systems.** Those that fail to direct water away from the foundation are a problem. Clogged gutters allow water to spill over and run down the siding toward the foundation wall. Leaders that dump water near the foundation encourage water to soak

in at exactly the wrong places. Use splash blocks or leader extensions to direct water away from the house.

**Improper Grading.** If the grading slopes toward the house or allows water to pool near the foundation, it is a problem. To conduct water away from the foundation, the grade must drop at least 6 inches in 10 feet all around the house. Fill in pockets that encourage water to pool.

**Lack of Footing Drains.** Some water inevitably reaches the bottom of the foundation but it will not be a problem if perforated pipes, called footing drains, lead it away. Most newer houses have footing drains but older homes may not. Drains can be added to older houses, though not without considerable effort. This is a job for a contractor. It involves the use of heavy equipment to excavate the entire perimeter of the foundation. It also involves the placement of gravel subdrains; the placement of perforated piping for the main drains; and finally, backfilling and regrading.

**Cracked Foundation Walls.** Water will get through even the smallest cracks, so use hydraulic cement to patch all of them.

**Pipes or Electrical Lines.** The problem is not the pipe or the line; it is the gap around the pipe and the line that leads water into the basement. Seal gaps with hydraulic cement or silicone sealant (a high-performance product similar to silicone caulk).

**Poorly Waterproofed Foundation.** A foundation such as this allows moisture to migrate directly through the masonry. Concrete and concrete block are not waterproof. The outside of every foundation wall is supposed to be waterproofed prior to backfilling. If the foundation was not waterproofed or if the waterproofing

failed, the solution is not something the novice is advised to attempt. Like installing new footing drains, a good bit of excavation is required.

**Nearby Vegetation.** Plants hold moisture in the soil and their shade reduces the evaporation of ground moisture. Both factors add to water woes. Another factor: plants that require a lot of deep watering add moisture to the soil that could seep in.

**High Water Table.** The water table varies in depth from area to area and even from season to season. Nothing can be done about the level, but foundation drains and sump pumps can help conduct water away before it becomes a problem.

## Sealing a Masonry Wall

Even if the basement is not plagued by the kind of water problems that show up as active drips, moisture still may be seeping through the masonry itself. This kind of moisture movement can be stopped by sealing the walls from inside the basement. Even if the walls seem to be "dry," sealing them is a reasonable precaution to take. After all, it does

not take much moisture to warp wood paneling or to encourage a musty smell. To seal the walls, brush them with a product that contains portland cement and synthetic rubber. This product goes by many names: cement paint, waterproofing paint, basement paint, or basement waterproofer. Though some brands claim to keep out water that is under a modest amount of pressure, nothing applied to the inside of the walls can solve serious water problems. After applying a waterproofing paint, paint over it with a quality latex paint.

**1** **Cleaning the Surfaces.** Use a wire brush to remove loose mortar and dirt from the walls. Sealing is most effective on a wall that has never been painted, but if all of the old paint is removed, the sealant still has a chance to do its job.

**2** **Removing Efflorescence.** A harmless, white, crystalline deposit called efflorescence sometimes forms on concrete or concrete-block walls. It is caused by water-soluble salts within the masonry that migrate to the wall's surface and interferes with the bond between the

**1** Use a scraper and a wire brush to remove loose mortar and dirt, and then vacuum the wall to remove the remaining dust and debris.

**2** Use a bristle brush and a mixture of etching compound and water to remove efflorescence on the surface of the masonry. Wear rubber gloves and eye protection.

waterproofing paint and the wall. A commercial etching compound that is dissolved in water and applied with a stiff bristle brush can be used to remove efflorescence. Etching compound contains a mild acid, however, so follow manufacturer's application and safety instructions to the letter. Rubber gloves and eye protection are mandatory. Use clean water to rinse the wall surface thoroughly so the acid is neutralized. Then let the wall dry thoroughly.

**3 Preparing Cracks and Holes.** Use a chisel to undercut cracks and holes slightly to provide a "key" that holds hydraulic cement in place. Hydraulic cement particularly is effective at sealing cracks where moisture is present, and because it expands slightly as it cures, it locks tightly to a properly prepared crack. After keying, vacuum the crack area to remove loose dust and debris.

**4 Applying Cement.** Mix a small amount of powdered hydraulic cement with water. If the leak is active, wait until the mixture becomes warm to the touch (indicating that it is beginning to set), and then use your hand, protected by a rubber glove, to force it into a portion of the crack. Hold the mixture in place for several minutes until it cures. If the leak is not active soak the area with water first,

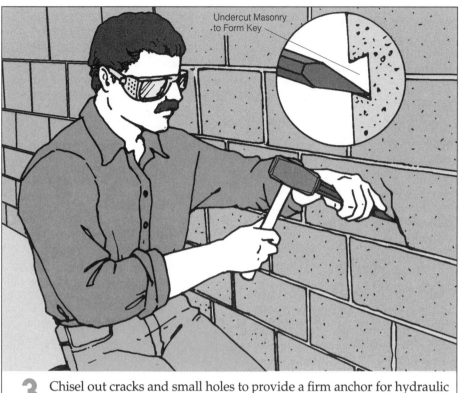

Undercut Masonry to Form Key

**3** Chisel out cracks and small holes to provide a firm anchor for hydraulic cement. Clean out debris. Use a hand-drilling hammer and cold chisel.

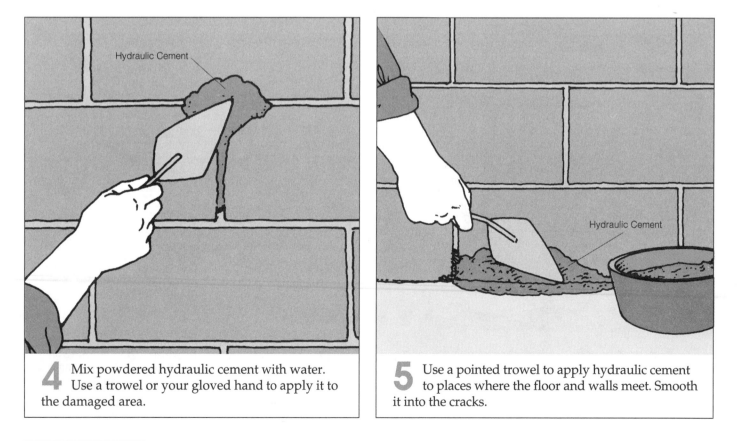

Hydraulic Cement

**4** Mix powdered hydraulic cement with water. Use a trowel or your gloved hand to apply it to the damaged area.

Hydraulic Cement

**5** Use a pointed trowel to apply hydraulic cement to places where the floor and walls meet. Smooth it into the cracks.

and then use a trowel to force the cement mixture into cracks and holes. Use the trowel to smooth out patched areas immediately.

**5** **Plugging Other Water Problems.** Water seepage also may be a problem at the juncture of floor slab and walls. Use a liberal amount of hydraulic cement to seal the area, and then smooth it with the trowel.

**6** **Applying Waterproofing Paint.** Once the hydraulic cement has cured and the wall is dry, use waterproofing paint to seal the walls. Make sure the work area is well ventilated. For best results use a wide nylon bristle brush to dab the material into the pores of the masonry. Allow the first coat to dry overnight, and then apply a second coat.

## Correcting Severe Water Problems

If water continues to enter the basement despite efforts to seal the walls from the inside, the problem must be tackled from the outside. If an excessive amount of water builds up in the soil just outside the foundation, it will be forced (by hydrostatic pressure) through the masonry. Water that is under a modest amount of pressure can be sealed out with waterproofing paint; however, large amounts of pressure can defeat any product that is applied to the inside of the wall. A waterproofing layer that is applied to the outside of the foundation is far more effective. This is because the more pressure is applied to it, the tighter the waterproofing adheres to the wall. However, it is not easy to waterproof the outside of the foundation, and it is not inexpensive. Because all possible strategies involve a good bit of excavation, this work is best left to a contractor. The work typically involves digging down to the footing, installing a system of drainpipes to redirect water around the house, and applying a protective waterproofing membrane to the outside of foundation walls. Compare several estimates before signing a contract.

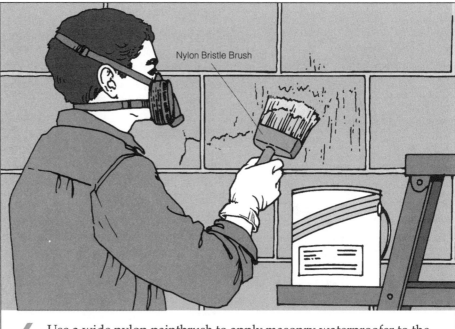

**6** Use a wide nylon paintbrush to apply masonry waterproofer to the walls. Work it into the rough surface of concrete block.

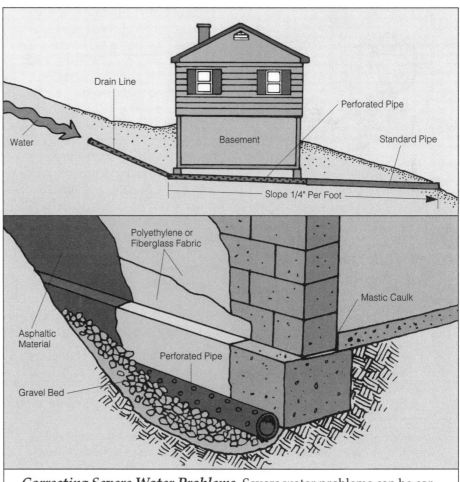

*Correcting Severe Water Problems.* Severe water problems can be corrected by intercepting water before it reaches the foundation (top) or by waterproofing the foundation itself (bottom), or both.

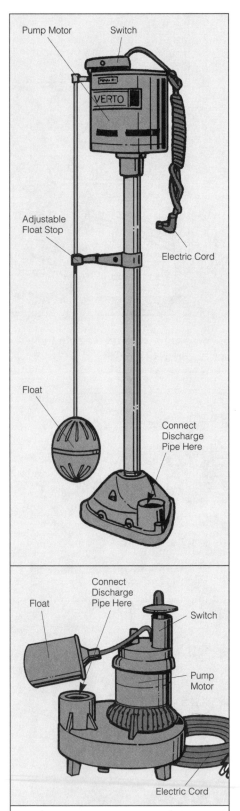

Pump Motor     Switch

VERTO

Adjustable
Float Stop

Electric Cord

Float

Connect
Discharge
Pipe Here

Connect
Discharge
Pipe Here

Float

Switch

Pump
Motor

Electric Cord

***Types of Sump Pumps.*** The pump motor on a pedestal pump (top) stays clear of the water. The pump motor on a submersible pump (bottom) is immersed in the water.

## Sump Pumps

One way to keep the basement dry is to install an electric sump pump. This device draws water from beneath the slab and pumps it away from the house. The pump sits in a hole, or sump, that extends below the slab. When water collects in the sump, the pump turns on automatically and removes the water through a plastic discharge pipe that exits the basement above grade.

The installation of a sump pump calls for wiring, plumbing, and concrete-demolition skills. A pump must not be the only thing standing between you and a flooded basement, however. After all, pumps do fail. A sump pump may be part of a strategy to keep water out, but if water problems are severe, footing drains may have to be installed as well.

**Types of Sump Pumps.** There are two basic types of sump pumps. A pedestal-type pump features a raised motor that does not come in contact with water. Instead, it sits on top of a plastic pipe that extends into the sump. Water rising in the sump causes the float to rise and turn on the pump. When the water level drops so does the float, turning off the pump. With a submersible pump, the entire pump sits at the bottom of the sump pit and is submerged every time the sump fills up with water. A float on the pump triggers the on-off switch. Either type of sump pump removes water effectively. Consult a plumber or a pump supplier to determine the best one for your particular situation.

## Installing a Sump Pump

In addition to plumbing codes, the pump installation must conform to electrical codes, which in general terms means that the pump must be supplied by a dedicated 15-amp circuit. The following step-by-step project is a guide to how the work usually is done but be sure to check local codes and the manufacturer's instructions that came with the pump. The exact dimensions of the sump pit,

for example, depend on the size of the liner (sometimes called a basin). Purchase the pump and the liner before starting work.

1 **Digging the Sump.** The sump pump is located in the lowest part of the basement so that water naturally drains to it. The whole point of installing the device is to keep water out of the basement to begin with, of course, but it is still prudent to locate the pump this way. Turn the basin upside down and use it as a template to scribe a circle on the floor; the circle's centerpoint must be about 16 inches away from both walls. Busting a hole in a 4-inch-thick slab is not easy work so rent an electric jackhammer or a heavy-duty rotary hammer for the job. Wear safety glasses and remove concrete up to the layout line. Then dig out the soil and gravel beneath the slab—the depth depends on the size of the liner (usually about 24 inches). Periodically slip the liner into place to see if it fits.

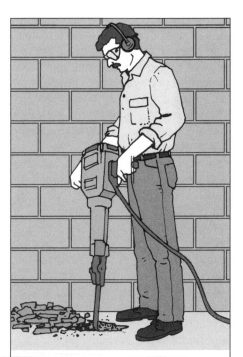

1 To reduce the amount of work involved in digging a sump, rent a jackhammer, as shown, or a rotary hammer. Be sure to wear safety glasses and hearing protection when using either tool.

**2** Slip the liner into place and fill in with gravel as needed.

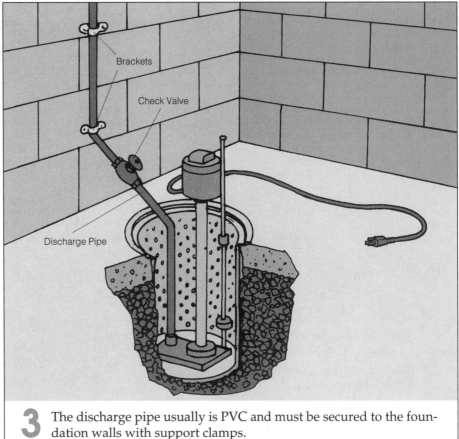

**3** The discharge pipe usually is PVC and must be secured to the foundation walls with support clamps.

**2** **Installing the Liner.** The liner is a plastic tub with holes in the sides that allow ground water to seep into it. Some liners have a lip at the top that covers the edges of the concrete. Once the hole is deep enough slip the liner into place, fill in around it as needed with gravel, and (if necessary) use hydraulic cement to seal the edges of the hole.

**3** **Connecting the Discharge Pipe.** Check the manufacturer's instructions that came with the pump to determine the type of discharge pipe needed and the necessary diameter (usually 1¼-inch PVC pipe). Attach a piece of pipe that is long enough to reach the pump itself (submersible type) or the intake housing (pedestal type). Then lower the pump into the sump and connect additional discharge pipe as needed. Support clamps must secure the pipe to the foundation walls and a check valve must be used somewhere in the discharge piping to keep water from draining back into the sump. If the pump has to be removed for servicing disconnect the discharge pipe at the check valve. It usually has a threaded fitting.

**4** **Cutting the Rim Joist.** It usually is easiest to route out the discharge piping through the rim joist. Afterwards, use caulk to seal the hole. Be sure that the end of the discharge pipe does not dump the water against the outside of the foundation walls. A splash block can be used to direct water.

**5** **Wiring and Testing the Pump.** Check local electrical codes to see if a ground-fault circuit interrupter (GFCI) is required for a sump pump, then run wiring from the service panel to the general location of the new pump. The pump itself has a long electrical cord and three-prong plug, so a grounded receptacle must be installed for it. This arrangement makes it easy to disconnect the pump should it ever need servicing. The box

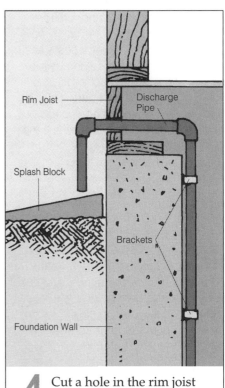

**4** Cut a hole in the rim joist and route the discharge pipe through it. Direct water away from the foundation wall.

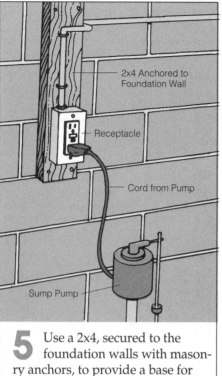

**5** Use a 2x4, secured to the foundation walls with masonry anchors, to provide a base for installing the electrical box.

typically is located high on a wall to avoid splashes caused by the pump itself. (Check local codes for specifics.) Use masonry anchors to secure a 2x4 to the foundation walls. (See page 36.) This provides a secure base for installing the electrical box. After installing the discharge pipe plug in the pump and pour water into the sump. The pump begins to work when the sump is about half full. As water flows through the discharge pipe, check all connections for leaks.

## Stairs

One advantage to adding new living space in the basement rather than the attic is that a stairway already is in place. It may be suitable just the way it is, but in some cases it must be rebuilt. Building codes are strict when it comes to stair construction, in part because small variations in details such as step height make a big difference in the safety of the stairs. For a basement conversion, you may decide to insulate the concrete floor with a system of wood sleepers and rigid insulation capped

## Basic Stair Dimensions

Your local building codes are the last word on stair dimensions but the following can be a guide.

■ The width of the stair must be at least 36 inches. Measure between finished walls.

■ Nosings (if used) must not project more than 1½ inches.

■ Headroom must measure at least 6 feet 8 inches from the tip of the nosing to the nearest obstruction at all points on the stair.

■ The ratio of riser height to tread depth should total 18 inches. The ideal riser height, for example, is 7 inches and the ideal tread depth is 11 inches (7 + 11 = 18). Risers must be no more than 8¼ inches high; treads must be at least 9 inches deep.

■ All stairs made up of three or more risers must have a 30- to 38-inch handrail on at least one side. Handrails are measured vertically from the tip of the tread nosing. The end of the handrail must return to the wall or terminate in a newel post.

■ Landings must be the same width as the stair and at least as long as they are wide.

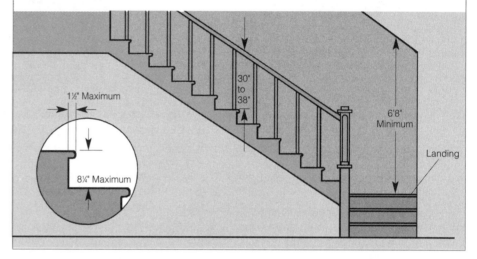

with plywood and carpeting. The thickness of this assembly changes the height of the last step on the stairs; it becomes shorter than all the others by the thickness of the new floor system. Unless this problem is corrected, the stairs will not be safe, and the project will not pass code inspection. Unfortunately, in this situation the stair carriage cannot simply be raised—the stairs have to be rebuilt. There are other reasons to rebuild a stairway, too. Though basement stairs in all newer houses have to adhere to the same codes as those anywhere else in the house, this was not always the case. If your house is an old one and the basement stairs are uncomfortably steep or poorly constructed, they must be rebuilt. Usually this can be done without

enlarging the stairwell itself. If it is necessary to build stairs, consult a reputable book on stair building (*Quick Guide: Stairs & Railings*, Creative Homeowner, $7.95).

### Adding a Balustrade

Many existing basement stairs may not be up to code. In particular, handrails and railings often are missing or inadequate. If the stairs are usable otherwise, however, handrails easily can be added to an existing stairway. Balusters are bolted directly to a stringer; bolts or screws can be countersunk and concealed with wood plugs. Space the balusters so that the opening between them is no more than 6 inches measured horizontally. The top of the handrail must be easy to grasp.

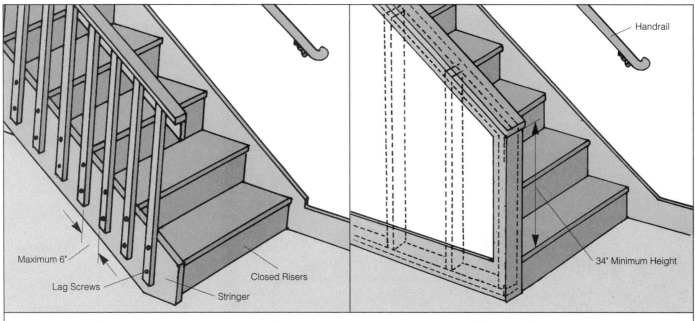

*Adding a Balustrade.* For an open balustrade (left), balusters must be fastened securely to the side of a stringer. A slanting partition wall (right) can be used to conceal part of the stair while retaining an open look.

Another option is to partly enclose the stairs on one side with a wall that follows the stairway pitch. A handrail can be placed either on the partial wall, on the full wall, or on both. The partial wall can be built just as if it were a partition wall with a slanted top plate. The stringer is securely fastened to the studs of the partition wall. Cover both sides of the new wall with drywall or paneling.

## Concealing Mechanical Equipment

A basement is packed with remodeling obstacles including sump pumps, water pumps, water heaters, pipes, ducts, drains, and furnaces, among other things. It is easiest to avoid these items from the start so try to work the design around them. If they cannot be avoided, however, often they can be concealed.

If the furnace shares space with basement living areas, safety is the most important issue to consider. The furnace is best located in a separate room, though it can share the space with other mechanical equipment such as the water softener and water heater. Local building codes may regulate the size and details of the room; check them for specifics. Generally, however, a furnace room must have a door that is big enough to remove the largest piece of equipment, though in no case can the door be less than 20 inches wide. The room must contain an unobstructed working space on the control side of the furnace that is at least 30 inches wide and 30 inches high. It also is a good idea to provide a light that is controlled by a switch near the door.

### Clearances For Heating Appliances

| Residential-Type Appliances | Clearance (inches) | | | |
|---|---|---|---|---|
| | Above Top* | From Front | From Back | From Sides |
| *Boilers & Water Heaters:* | | | | |
| Automatic oil or combination gas & oil | 6 | 24 | 6 | 6 |
| Automatic gas | 6 | 18 | 6 | 6 |
| Solid | 6 | 48 | 6 | 6 |
| Electric | 6 | 18 | 6 | 6 |
| *Central Furnaces:* | | | | |
| Automatic oil or combination gas & oil | 6 | 24 | 6 | 6 |
| Automatic gas | 6 | 18 | 6 | 6 |
| Solid | 18 | 48 | 18 | 18 |
| Electric | 6 | 18 | 6 | 6 |

\* Same clearances required from top and sides of warm air bonnet or plenum of central furnaces.

This chart illustrates approximate clearances to maintain between heating appliances and a combustible wall. **Check your local building codes.**

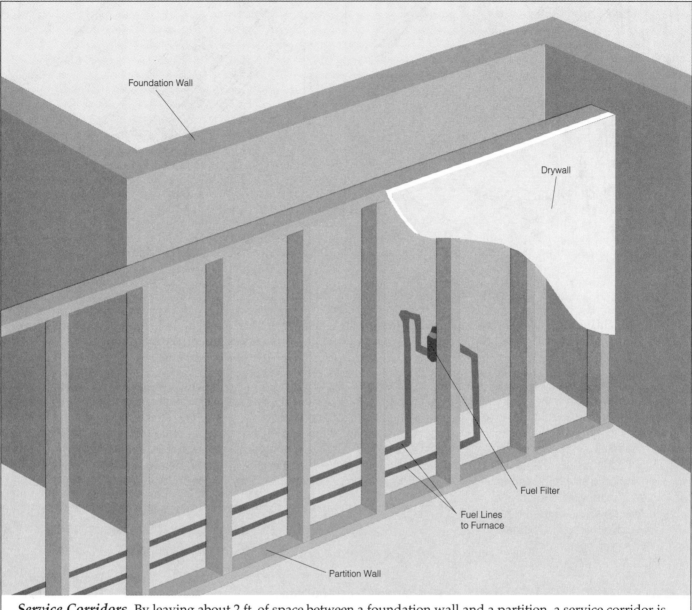

*Service Corridors.* By leaving about 2 ft. of space between a foundation wall and a partition, a service corridor is created and allows for easy access to various devices.

Be sure to vent the room so that there is enough incoming air for a combustion-type furnace. The amount of air required depends on the type and capacity of the furnace; check with a local heating contractor.

As a safety precaution (particularly if someone is to sleep in the basement even occasionally) install a carbon monoxide detector. Carbon monoxide is a colorless, odorless, and potentially lethal gas that is a by-product of combustion. Under normal circumstances carbon monoxide is vented

out of the house, but a faulty furnace or gas water heater may cause it to leak into the basement. A detector sounds an alarm when it senses carbon monoxide.

Building codes regulate the distance between heating appliances and combustible walls so check local codes before building a room for the furnaces and other appliances. In the meantime, however, the chart "Clearances For Heating Appliances" (see page 27) provides an idea of what is required.

**Service Corridors.** Combustion furnaces are supplied with fuel via fuel lines. These fuel lines have a fuel filter that must be accessible for periodic maintenance. Fuel lines must never run beneath flooring but can be hidden behind a partition wall. By leaving about 24 inches between the partition wall and the foundation, a service corridor is created and can be used for ready access to the line. A service corridor also can be used to maintain access to other devices, such as a sump pump or a water pump.

# FLOOR REPAIR & PREPARATION

A smooth, unblemished floor is an asset to any basement remodeling project. Cracks must be repaired even if you plan to install an insulated subfloor, and particularly if you plan to paint the floor. An insulated subfloor keeps the room cozy.

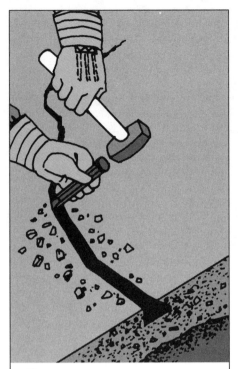

**1** Use a cold chisel to enlarge the crack. Undercut the crack slightly to provide a key for the patching compound.

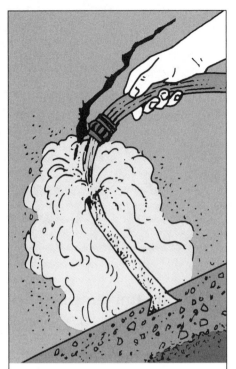

**2** Vacuum the crack to remove debris, then flush it with water to prevent dry concrete from wicking moisture away from the patching cement. Remove traces of dust and debris.

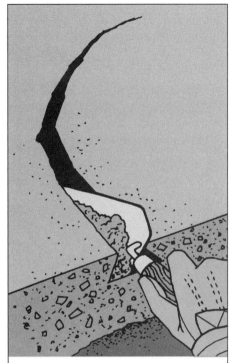

**3** Use the edge of the trowel to pack the patching cement into the crack. Then smooth the cement flush with the surrounding surface.

# Repairing a Concrete Floor

It is a rare to find a floor slab completely free of cracks and damage. Minor cracking and small areas of damage are handled easily, though larger areas may call for partial removal of the slab and the advice of a contractor. In any case, repairs must be made before a subfloor or a finished floor is added. Always use safety goggles and gloves when removing concrete or working with patching products.

## Repairing Cracks

Cracks up to 3/8 inch wide can be patched with hydraulic cement. If you have wider cracks you probably have serious foundation problems and should consult a foundation contractor. Hydraulic cement sets in 3 to 5 minutes, so mix up only what you can use in that amount of time and

clean up overspread material promptly. It is wise to wear gloves when handling cement.

**1** **Clearing the Crack.** If the crack is wide enough that the blade of a cold chisel fits into it, open it up and undercut the sides so that the beveled edges anchor the patch. A cold chisel, made of less brittle steel than a wood chisel, is designed for masonry work. Use a wire brush to remove loose debris from the edges of the undercut area, then vacuum out the debris and dust. Use hydraulic cement to make the patch itself.

**2** **Preparing the Crack.** Before using some brands of hydraulic cement, the area to be patched must be soaked with water to keep the concrete from wicking moisture away from the patch. Once the standing water has been absorbed by the concrete, proceed with the patch. Follow instructions found on the manufacturer's label.

**3** **Filling the Crack.** Mix a batch of hydraulic cement and force it into the damaged area. Use the edge of a trowel to tamp the material into

### Floor Overlays

If the surface of the slab has minor damage over a wide area, or if the surface is too rough to serve as a finished floor, it can be topped with a new surface. Overlay compound is a gypsum-based liquid product that is self-leveling. It is poured over the floor to a thickness of up to 1/2 inch and spread with a floor squeegee. The floor, when fully cured, is smooth and uniform. Follow instructions on the product label. Note that it is necessary to contain the product as it is being installed to keep it from flowing into drains.

place, then use the flat surface of the trowel to level and smooth the patch.

# Painting a Concrete Floor

Paint is an excellent choice for those who want to keep remodeling costs way down or if the basement simply will be used as a workshop. A painted floor prevents stains from reaching the concrete itself, making them easier to clean up. It also seals the surface against dusting, a powdery residue that sometimes forms on the surface of the concrete. A properly prepared concrete surface, along with the right type of paint, ensures success.

Concrete gains most of its strength soon after being poured but continues to cure for years afterwards. If the house is new let the concrete cure for at least two years before painting it. Make sure moisture problems found in an older house are solved before the floor is painted. (See page 20.)

## Concrete Paints

The paint used on a concrete floor must be abrasion-resistant and have the same rate of expansion and contraction as the concrete itself. Epoxy-based paint fits this description, though it can be expensive and difficult to apply. Its durability and high bonding strength make it a suitable product to use on floors that are expected to receive wear and tear. Masonry paint, on the other hand, is compatible, durable, and relatively inexpensive. It has a latex base and forms a tough skin that resists abrasion as well as the alkaline chemistry of concrete. Yet another product, called cement paint (regardless of its name), is not suitable for cement floors. It is used to seal walls and cannot withstand foot traffic.

## Painting the Floor

An etching liquid is used to rough up a smooth, shiny surface. This product contains a mild acid, however, so

**Painting the Floor.** Pour a modest amount of paint directly onto the floor and spread it with a roller. Keep the leading edge of the painted area wet so the roller strokes blend together. Don't paint yourself into a corner.

follow the manufacturer's application and safety instructions to the letter. Rubber gloves and eye protection are mandatory. If the concrete already feels slightly rough to the touch, use trisodium phosphate (TSP) or a phosphate-free cleaner to clean stains and heavily soiled areas. Just before painting, vacuum the floor to remove dust. Pour modest amounts of paint directly onto the floor and then use a medium-nap roller to spread it. The idea is to keep the leading edge of the painted area wet so the roller strokes blend together. Spread it evenly, otherwise the paint will not dry properly. Apply a second coat after the first is dry (usually within 24 hours).

# Installing an Insulated Subfloor

Most likely, there is no insulation beneath your basement slab (one exception might be an unfinished daylight basement where at least

one wall is exposed to the grade). Contact the builder, if possible, to determine if insulation exists. An uninsulated slab is uncomfortably cold in the winter.

An insulated subfloor isolates the finished floor from the slab, resulting in a warmer floor and helping to prevent moisture from damaging the finished flooring. The insulated subfloor consists of plywood that is nailed to sleepers (2x4s laid flat). Rigid insulation fits between the sleepers. Subflooring plywood comes in two edge configurations: square edge and tongue-and-groove edge. Either configuration can be used for a basement subfloor but tongue-and-groove plywood eliminates the need for blocks placed beneath unsupported edges of the plywood. Remember, there must be at least 90 inches of headroom (84 inches in kitchens, hallways, and bathrooms) after the insulated subfloor has been installed.

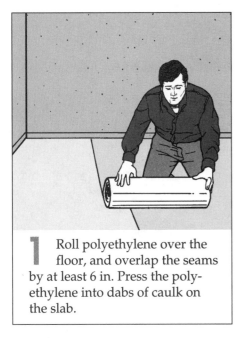

**1** Roll polyethylene over the floor, and overlap the seams by at least 6 in. Press the polyethylene into dabs of caulk on the slab.

**1 Putting Down a Vapor Barrier.** After sweeping the floor slab, cover it with 6-mil polyethylene. Overlap each seam by a minimum of 6 inches. Lift up the edges of the polyethylene, and use a caulking gun to put down dabs of caulk to hold it in place.

**2 Installing Perimeter Sleepers.** Use 2¼-inch-long masonry nails to nail sleepers around the perimeter of the room. If the lumber is dry and straight, a nail or two installed every several feet suffices. Mark these perimeter sleepers for additional sleepers 24 inches on center. This spacing is suitable for 3/4-inch plywood.

**3 Installing Interior Sleepers.** Align the interior sleepers square

to the marks on the perimeter sleepers. Use one nail at the end of each board and one about every 4 feet. If one sleeper does not extend completely across the room butt two sleepers end to end.

**4 Inserting Foam.** Medium density extruded polystyrene foam is best for concrete floor slabs. Use a thickness that matches the thickness of the sleepers. Cut each piece to fit between the sleepers, and insert them.

**5 Attaching the Subfloor.** Use 3/4-inch-plywood subflooring (straightedge or tongue-and-groove). Cut the plywood to span across, rather than parallel to, the sleepers. Start alternate courses with half-sheets of plywood to stagger end joints.

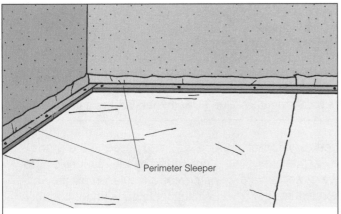

Perimeter Sleeper

**2** Nail sleepers around the perimeter of the room, butting joints as needed. The pieces must be straight and flat. Use masonry nails spaced every few feet to secure them to the slab.

Hand-Drilling Hammer

**3** Space 2x4 sleepers 24 in. on center. Align them to provide solid bearing for the plywood, and then nail them to the floor.

**4** Cut rigid foam to fit between the sleepers, and drop it in place.

Plywood Half-Sheet

**5** Use 6d nails to attach plywood to the sleepers. Drive the nails at 6-in. intervals into the end supports of each panel and 12 in. over intermediate supports.

# FRAMING & INSULATING WALLS

The necessity of working on masonry walls and on concrete floors is what makes remodeling a basement so different from remodeling other areas of the house. With a few specialized tools and materials, it is possible to build basement walls and insulate a new room with ease.

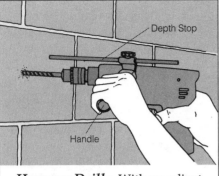

**Hammer Drills.** With an adjustable depth stop and auxiliary handle, hammer drills can be used with accuracy.

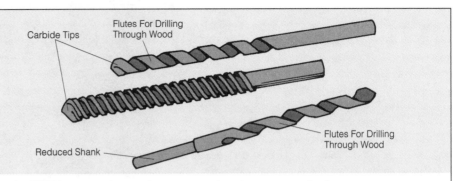

**Drill Bits.** The flutes of a masonry bit determine whether or not it can be used to drill directly through wood into masonry (top and bottom). The reduced shank of some masonry bits allows them to be used in standard 3/8-in. drills (bottom).

# Fastening Objects to Masonry

In the course of most basement remodeling projects, something will have to be fastened to a masonry surface. For instance, shelf-support brackets or furring strips might have to be installed on concrete block walls or the bottom plate of a partition wall might have to be nailed into a concrete floor. The task of fastening objects to masonry calls for special tools, fasteners, and techniques. It also calls for a protective dust mask and eye protection as the process creates an abundance of fine, abrasive dust.

**Hammer Drills.** A power drill is indispensable when it comes to drilling into masonry. Consider buying or renting a hammer drill if many holes have to be drilled. This tool creates a hammering motion as the bit spins. The dual action helps shatter aggregate in the concrete and clear dust from the hole.

**Drill Bits.** A bit designed for use in masonry is recognizable by its enlarged carbide tip and unusually wide flutes. Though more brittle than steel, carbide holds up well to the abrasive process of drilling into masonry. The wide flutes help to clear dust and debris away from the hole. Bits with "fast-spiral" flutes are the ones most commonly seen in hardware stores and home centers but they are not suitable for drilling through wood and into masonry in one pass (as when setting wall plates). In this case use a masonry bit with regular "twist" flutes. Some masonry bits have reduced shanks that fit into 3/8-inch drills.

Not all masonry bits, however, can be used in a hammer drill. The percussive action can damage or destroy some grades of carbide. Make sure the masonry bit used in the hammer drill is approved specifically for this use—look for a note on the packaging.

## Drilling into Masonry

**1** **Marking the Depth.** Every fastener has a different depth requirement. If the drill has a depth stop, set it so time is not wasted drilling deeper than necessary. If the

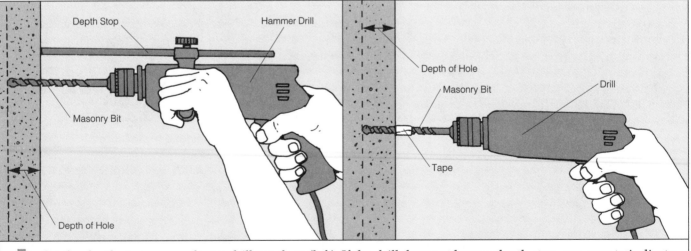

**1** Set the depth stop so you do not drill too deep (left). If the drill does not have a depth stop, one way to indicate depth is to wrap tape around the bit. Stop drilling when the tape reaches the surface of the masonry (right).

Location Mark

**2** Hold the drill at a right angle to the masonry and use a slow speed to get the drill bit started.

Turkey Baster

**3** All dust must be removed from the hole before an anchor or other fastener is installed. Wear eye protection when clearing out a hole.

drill does not have a stop fasten a piece of masking tape to the bit as a visual reminder of how deep to drill.

**2** **Drilling the Hole.** Mark the location of the hole with a large "X" as a visual cue to keep the bit on target. Hold the drill in place and check to see that it is perpendicular to the surface. While wearing gloves (to cushion your hands from the percussive motion of a hammer drill) press the bit firmly against the surface to keep it from skating away from the mark. Then start the drill at a very slow speed. As the bit begins to work into the surface increase the speed and pressure gradually until the tip of the bit is immersed completely in the hole. Then maintain steady, firm pressure on the drill. Drill at a relatively slow speed to keep the bit from overheating. The depth stop halts progress at the proper depth. When drilling into a floor, back the spinning bit out of the hole frequently to help excavate dust and debris.

**3** **Cleaning the Hole.** Remove all dust from the hole. It might be tempting to lean close and blow out the dust but usually this results in a face full of grit. Use a rubber ear-

## Clearing the Hole

If, while drilling into concrete, progress stops before the hole is deep enough, it may be that the bit has hit a large piece of aggregate or a length of steel reinforcing bar (rebar). Pull the bit out of the hole and scrutinize the tip. If there are pieces of metal on it, the bit has hit rebar and a new hole has to be started nearby. There is no way to drill through rebar. If aggregate is the source of the slowdown shatter it with a hand-drilling hammer and a punch before resuming drilling. A hand-drilling hammer looks something like a miniature sledge hammer but its head is specially designed for striking concrete nails and metal implements. While wearing safety glasses, place the punch in the hole and strike it repeatedly with the hand-drilling hammer until the aggregate shatters.

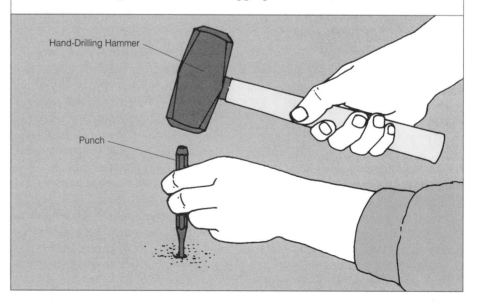

Hand-Drilling Hammer

Punch

syringe or a turkey baster instead to blow debris out of the hole. Keep your face well away from the action and wear eye protection.

## Masonry Fasteners

At one time, the choice for securing anything to masonry was limited to lead anchors. These days, however, there are many products from which to choose. Nearly all of them fall into one of two broad categories: mechanical anchors that grip the masonry, or chemical anchors that bond to it. For most fastening jobs encountered in the course of a basement remodeling project, mechanical anchors do quite nicely and generally are less expensive and more widely available than chemical anchors.

**Lead Sleeve Anchors.** The type of masonry anchor that most people know (and few love) is called a lead anchor. It consists of a lag bolt and a lead sleeve that fits into a hole that is drilled in the masonry. When the bolt is turned into the sleeve, the sleeve expands and grips the side of the hole. These fasteners are readily available and inexpensive but their holding power is limited. Another disadvantage is that two holes have to be drilled: a fairly large hole in the masonry (for the anchor) and a smaller one in the piece to be fastened (for the lag bolt). Use them to install shelf cleats or in other situations where the bolts are not subjected to a lot of pulling force (particularly if only a handful of fasteners are needed).

**Plastic Sleeve Anchors.** A better sleeve-type anchor has a plastic sleeve instead of a lead sleeve. Though two different sized holes still must be drilled (one in the masonry and one in the workpiece) the hole for the sleeve usually is smaller than the one required for a lead anchor (a distinction that makes a big difference if there are many anchors to install). A more important advantage, however, is that a plastic anchor holds better than a lead anchor. That makes them a better choice

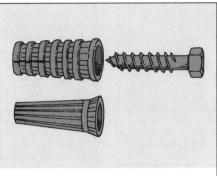

***Lead Sleeve Anchors.*** Lead sleeves are available in one- and two-piece versions.

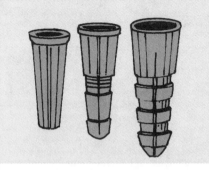

***Plastic Sleeve Anchors.*** These are slightly tapered and hold better than lead sleeves.

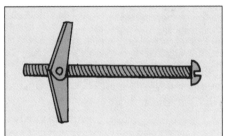

***Hollow-Wall Anchors.*** The "wings" of a hollow-wall anchor fold flat against the bolt so that the assembly can be inserted through a hole in concrete block.

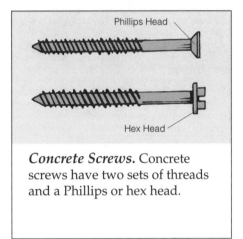

Phillips Head

Hex Head

***Concrete Screws.*** Concrete screws have two sets of threads and a Phillips or hex head.

for hanging heavy objects, such as cabinetry, from a masonry surface.

**Note:** When using either plastic or lead anchors, the depth of the hole is important to consider. It must be just slightly deeper than the length of the anchor. If it is too shallow, the anchor cannot seat properly and will not hold as well.

**Hollow-Wall Anchors.** When working with concrete block, usually it is best to drill right into the solid web of the block. This area offers the greatest holding power for sleeve-type fasteners. However, it may not be possible to guess where the web is located, or a fastener may be needed in a place where there is no web. In such cases, it is best to use a hollow wall anchor (sometimes called a toggle bolt). The most common version features a set of spring-loaded "wings" that are threaded to fit around a bolt. After the wings are

slipped through a hole, they expand and grip the backside of the hole as the bolt is tightened. These fasteners are inexpensive but can be awkward to use—once the wings are in the hole, the bolt cannot be withdrawn without losing the wings inside the wall.

**Concrete Screws.** Though it seems implausible, certain types of specially hardened screws can be driven directly into concrete or concrete block without requiring a sleeve. These screws, often referred to by the brand name, Tapcon, actually cut threads in the masonry. After drilling a pilot hole, simply turn the screw into the hole as if it was a wood screw. Though they are relatively expensive and not universally available, concrete screws are well worth the effort it takes to obtain them. They hold as well as most sleeve-type anchors and do not require two separately sized holes.

**Masonry Nails.** For speedy installation nothing beats a masonry nail. These fasteners have a thicker shank and heavier head than a standard nail of the same length; they also have flutes that lock into the masonry. When nailing into concrete, the work goes easier if the concrete has been poured within the last 30 days or so; fully-cured concrete requires more elbow grease. Though the holding power of a masonry nail is not great, they are easy to install so you can use more of them. They particularly are useful when securing wood cleats to a wall and when fastening wall plates to a concrete floor. Masonry nails also can be used on concrete block walls but they should be nailed into the mortar joint rather than the blocks themselves.

**Hand-Drilling Hammer.** Because masonry nails are treated with heat in a special process called "hardening," they do not bend as they are driven into masonry. Hardening,

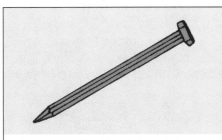

***Masonry Nails.*** This nail has a fluted shaft and is hardened to resist bending.

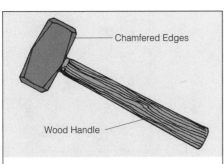

Chamfered Edges

Wood Handle

***Hand-Drilling Hammer.*** The extra heft and special head of this hammer make it the best (and safest) for striking masonry nails. Always wear eye protection when working with masonry nails.

### Using Masonry Nails

It takes a special touch to drive masonry nails into a masonry surface, particularly if the surface is concrete. First of all, wear safety glasses and be sure to use a hand-drilling hammer rather than a standard one. Do not use nails that will penetrate more than 1 inch into the concrete—a nail longer than necessary is harder to drive and increases the chance of damaging the concrete. Make sure that the nail is perpendicular to the surface, and then gradually drive it into the wood. When you feel the nail reach the concrete beneath, strike harder, letting the weight of the hammer's head rest against the nail at the end of each blow. Do not let the hammer "bounce" off the nailhead; it will be more difficult to strike the nail squarely with the next blow.

however, means that masonry nails must never be driven with a standard hammer—the nails are likely to damage the hammer head which can send razor-sharp metal shards into the air. Use a hand-drilling hammer or a ball peen hammer instead.

***Caution:*** *When working with masonry nails, wear eye protection to protect yourself from flying metal and masonry chips.*

### Chemical Anchors

Though a mechanical anchor handles most fastening tasks, in special situations a chemical anchor is needed (such as where the hole has to be made at the edge of a concrete block). Unlike chemical anchors, most mechanical anchors stress the masonry around a hole so they are more likely to cause the masonry to crumble. The various chemical products work in similar ways. A hole is drilled in the masonry, filled with an epoxy-like mixture and then a threaded rod is pushed into the hole and held in place until the adhesive sets. Some adhesives can be mixed thick enough to resist dripping when used on a vertical surface. Chemical anchors, though relatively expensive, tenaciously grip the masonry. They usually are available at larger hardware and home center stores.

Another anchoring product is called hydraulic cement, though it typically is used to patch masonry. This fast-setting cement expands slightly as

it cures and has more compressive strength than standard concrete. It can be mixed to a stiff consistency to stay on a vertical surface or to a more liquid consistency for use on floors. Drill a hole in the masonry, remove the dust, pack the hole with cement and imbed a fastener or anchor. This product often is used when a fastener has to be placed in a damaged portion of masonry.

## Partition Walls

The wide open space of a full basement is perfect for a pool table or play area, but if the basement is going to be used for something else, it may be better subdivided into smaller areas. A partition is a wall that separates rooms. It is used to enclose a bathroom or to split the basement into a recreation room and storage area. The same framing technique also is used to build secondary walls (see page 42). In any case, it is much easier to attach finished wall surfaces to wooden framing than to masonry walls.

Structural walls (those that are load-bearing) transfer loads from one part of the house to the foundation. But if partition walls are being added to a basement, they will be nonbearing. That is, they will be attached to the basement floor and to the underside of the ceiling joists and will not carry loads other than the weight of whatever is fastened to them. In most cases, it is possible to build the partitions one at a time on the basement floor and then raise them into place. Where space is limited or where obstructions such as pipes or beams make it hard to raise a partition, they can be assembled in place.

If a partition wall will run perpendicular to the joists, all that has to be done to anchor the top of the wall is to shim and nail through the plate into the joists (using 12d nails). If the wall will run parallel to the joists, install 2x4 blocking between the

joists to provide a nailer. Blocks usually are set 16 inches on center but in this case they are offset from the partition studs to make it possible to nail into them through the partition plate with a pair of 12d nails.

### Building a Tip-Up Partition

After the floors have been painted, subfloors have been installed, and moisture-proofing is done on the foundation walls, partition walls can be tipped up into place. Partition walls typically are built with 2x4 lumber and have a single top and bottom plate. Because it is not structural, the prime requirement of a partition wall is that it suitably supports finished wall surfaces.

**1** **Marking the Location.** Mark the exact location of the bottom plate on the floor. Use a framing square and straightedge to ensure square corners and a chalkline to ensure straight lines. If working alone, wedge one end of the chalkline under a weight to hold it as the other end is snapped (it is easier to have a helper hold one end).

**2** **Laying out the Plates.** Cut two plates to the length of the partition. Align the plates and measure

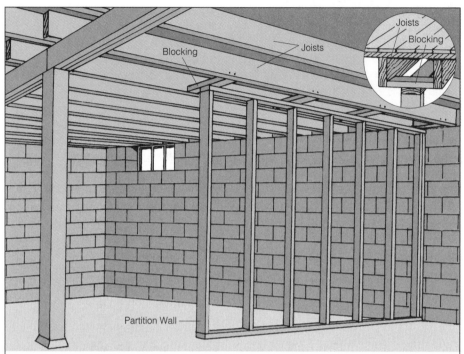

***Partition Walls.*** If a partition wall runs parallel to the joists secure its top plate to 2x4 blocking nailed between the joists.

**1** Determine the location of the wall. Then snap chalk lines on the floor to provide a layout.

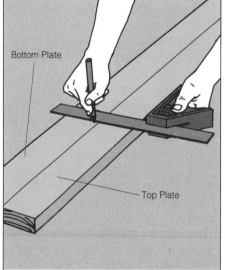

**2** Mark the bottom plate for the location of studs 16 in. on center. Then use a square to duplicate the layout marks on the top plate.

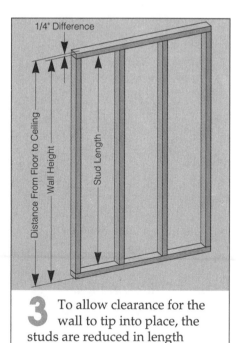

**3** To allow clearance for the wall to tip into place, the studs are reduced in length by 1/4 in.

Stud

Plate

**4** Assemble the wall piece by piece, nailing into each stud through the top and bottom plates. Make sure the edges of studs and plates are in the same plane.

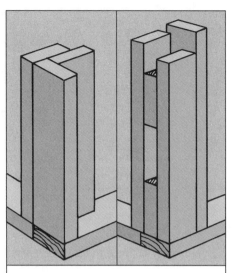

**5** In the places where two walls meet, frame the corner in such a way that there is adequate backing for the drywall on both the inside and the outside of the corner.

**6** Once the wall is fully assembled, tip it up and use the layout marks to align it. When it is in position use concrete nails (or common nails if a wood subfloor exists) to nail it to the floor.

from one end, marking for studs at 16-inch intervals on center (the standard spacing for studs). Continue to the other end of the plates even if the last stud is less than 16 inches from the end. To check your work, measure to a point exactly 4 feet from the starting end of the plates; done correctly, that point will be centered on one of the stud locations.

**3** **Cutting the Studs.** Wall studs are the height of the wall minus twice the thickness of the lumber (to account for the thickness of the plates). Subtract an additional 1/4 inch from this figure to provide enough clearance to raise the partition. Cut all the studs that are needed. (To come up with this number simply count the number of layout marks on either plate.) In order for the wall to fit properly, the cuts must be square.

**4** **Building the Frame.** Separate the plates by the length of a stud, and set them on edge with layout marks facing inward. Lay all studs in approximate position, and then drive a pair of 16d nails through each plate and into the ends of each stud. Use the marks as guides to precisely align the studs.

**5** **Forming a Corner.** To provide a nailing surface for drywall, add an extra stud to each end of the wall that forms an outside corner. One method of making the corner involves nailing spacers between two studs, then butting the end stud of the adjacent wall to this triple-width assembly. Another method is to use a stud to form the inside corner of the wall.

**6** **Raising the Wall.** This is done by sliding the bottom plate into approximate position (using the subfloor layout lines made in Step 1), then tipping the wall upright. Using a helper to prevent the wall from toppling over, align the bottom plate with the layout lines. Once the wall is in the proper location nail the bottom plate to the floor. When nailing the plate to a concrete floor use a single masonry nail set every 18 inches or so. If a wood subfloor already is in place use the longest common nails possible to nail into the subfloor without hitting the concrete. Nail into the sleepers wherever possible. Space the nails in pairs every 24 inches or so.

**7** **Plumbing the Wall.** Use a carpenter's level to ensure that the partition is plumb, and then add

Top Plate

Level

**7** Place a level against the edge of a wall stud and plumb the wall. Check the wall in several locations before nailing through the top plate and into the ceiling framing. Do not forget to shim.

shims between the top plate and each intersecting joist to take up the 1/4-inch clearance. Do not overshim—by doing so the joists may be raised or the top plate may be bent. Just make sure the partition is wedged snugly in place and that it is square. Then nail through the top plate and shims and into the ceiling framing (or into blocking if the wall is running parallel to the ceiling framing).

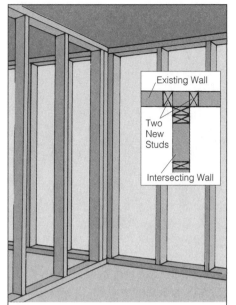

8 Frame the intersection of two walls so there is a full-length stud on either side of the intersection. The studs provide a backing as well as a nailing surface for the drywall.

**8 Joining Intersecting Walls.** In places where partition walls intersect, additional studs are installed to provide support for drywall. Add a single stud to the end of the intersecting wall. Add a pair of studs to the other wall. Use 16d nails to secure the intersections.

## Building a Partition in Place

It is not always possible to raise a partition wall. For example, pipes or ducts may be in the way, or the wall may be unusually long. Instead, partition walls can be built in place by slipping each stud between plates that have been nailed to the floor and ceiling joists. There are various ways to do this but the following method minimizes error:

**1 Installing the Top Plate.** First cut both plates to the length of the partition wall, and mark the top one for the position of studs (16 inches on center). Determine where the wall will go, and use a 16d nail to attach the top plate to each intersecting joist (or to blocking between the joists). Be sure that the stud layout faces down.

1 Mark the top plate for the stud spacing of the partition, and then nail the plate to the underside of the joists.

2 Use a plumb bob to lay out the position of the bottom plate directly beneath the top plate at at least two places on the floor. Then align the bottom plate to the layout lines.

**2 Locating the Bottom Plate.** Hang a plumb bob from the edge of the top plate, transferring the position of the top plate to at least two points on the floor as shown. Align the bottom plate with these layout marks and nail it to the floor. Use a single masonry nail every 18 inches or so if nailing to a concrete floor, or pairs of common nails every 24 inches if nailing to a wood subfloor.

**3 Installing the Studs.** Measure between the plates at each stud location, and cut studs to fit. (They will be the same length unless the floor or the joists are not exactly level.) Put a stud in position, align it with the layout marks, and use a pair of 12d nails to toenail it to the top plate. To make toenailing easier, use a spacer block to keep the stud from shifting as it is toenailed. Cut the

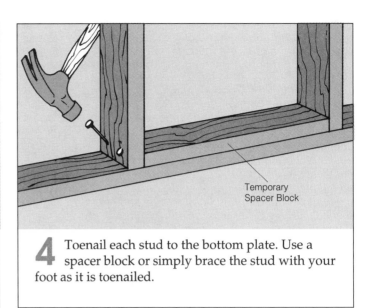

**3** Measure between the plates at each stud location and cut studs to fit. Toenail each stud to the top plate. Use a temporary spacer block to brace the end of a stud as it is nailed.

**4** Toenail each stud to the bottom plate. Use a spacer block or simply brace the stud with your foot as it is toenailed.

block to fit exactly between studs. (If the stud spacing is 16 inches on center and the studs are exactly 1½ inch thick, the block will be 14½ inches long.) Remove the spacer as successive studs are toenailed.

**4 Completing the Wall.** Plumb each stud and toenail it to the bottom plate—the same spacer block can be used. If you are installing the partition directly over a concrete floor, make sure the toenails do not hit the concrete. Use three 8d nails, and start the toenailing high enough on the stud so that the end of the nail stops short of the concrete.

## Insulating the Walls

The basement is the coolest part of the house during the winter and summer. The temperature does not vary much because basement walls are protected from temperature extremes by tons of earth. That coolness feels great on a hot summer day, but in order to be comfortable in cold weather, most basements require a supplementary heat source. (See page 16.) Unless the foundation walls are insulated, much of that supplementary heat is wasted. All walls that face unheated space, such as the partition between a basement recreation room and an unheated basement shop, must be insulated.

There are two basic ways to insulate the foundation walls, and each one calls for a different kind of insulation. Most likely it will not be necessary to install insulation that is higher in R-value than R-11. Check with local building officials to determine the amount of insulation that is recommended in your area.

### Insulating with Fiberglass

One way to insulate a foundation wall is to build a secondary 2x4 wall between it and the living space. This nonbearing wall can be insulated with R-11 fiberglass batts and blankets and finished the same as other framed walls. Install it after the wood subfloor is installed.

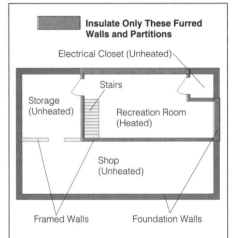

*Insulating the Walls.* Weatherstripped doors and insulated walls separate heated and unheated basement rooms.

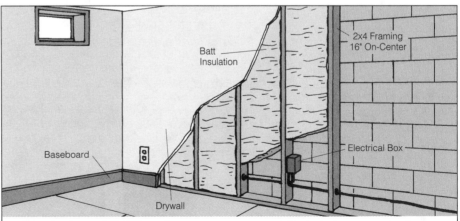

*Insulating with Fiberglass.* A 2x4 frame wall placed against the foundation walls is a good way to provide insulation. It also is a convenient route for wiring and plumbing runs.

**1** Stretch a string across each wall to make sure it is not bowed.

**2** Snap a chalkline to mark the front face of the stud wall. Position it so that the wall, when installed, is plumb and straight. It must stand clear of high spots on the wall.

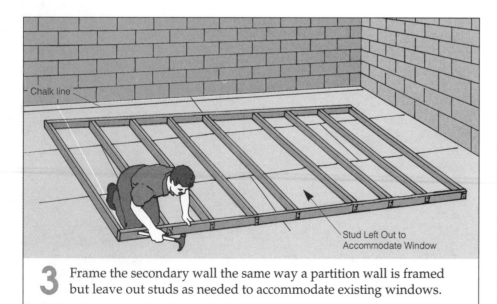

**3** Frame the secondary wall the same way a partition wall is framed but leave out studs as needed to accommodate existing windows.

If there is no subfloor, install the wall directly over the concrete. One advantage of building a secondary wall is that it is easy to install wiring (particularly electrical boxes) and plumbing runs into it. Also, installing the insulation is just as easy as installing it in a standard partition. On the negative side, however, a secondary wall takes up floor space that already may be in short supply. Extra care must be taken in detailing the framing around windows and doors that are located in basement stud walls.

Before the secondary walls are built make sure the foundation walls are free from moisture problems. Patch all cracks and use masonry waterproofer to seal the walls (see page 21). Moisture that collects behind the framing eventually leads to problems that are difficult to correct.

**1** **Checking the Foundation.** A secondary wall can rest directly against the foundation wall, but not all foundation walls are perfectly plumb and straight. To assess the situation use a 3-foot (or longer) level to make sure the walls are plumb. Then, with an assistant holding one end, stretch a string across the length of the wall and hold it about 3/4 inch away from the wall at each end. If the wall touches the the string, it is bowed inward; if the gap between string and wall is greater than 3/4 inch, the wall is bowed outward.

**2** **Laying out the Secondary Wall.** The framework is positioned so that it is straight and plumb. This might mean that in some places it has to stand slightly away from the foundation wall. Locate the innermost line, and then measure 3½ inches in and snap a chalkline to represent the face (the side drywall will be attached to) of the studs.

**3** **Framing the Wall.** A secondary wall is framed the same way a basement partition is framed, including the 1/4-inch clearance that enables the walls to be tipped into place. In other words cut the studs so they are 3¼ inches less than the distance between floor and joists. If there is a window in the foundation wall, adjust the layout so that there is one stud on either side of it. For the moment, leave out the framing between these two studs.

**4** **Shimming the Top Plate.** When the framework is assembled, raise it and align it with the layout marks on the floor. Have an assistant hold one end while you stretch a string across the length of the wall. Hold the string about 3/4 inch away from the studs at each end. If the wall touches the string, it is bowed inward; if the gap between string and framework is greater than 3/4 inch, the wall is bowed outward. Use wood shingles to shim between the top plate and the underside of each joist. Make sure the wall is plumb, and then nail through the top plate and into the joists using two 12d nails at each location.

**5** **Nailing the Bottom Plate.** Once the top plate is securely fastened to the joists, check the position of the bottom plate against layout lines, and double-check the studs for plumb. Then nail through the bottom plate as if nailing a partition wall.

**6** **Framing the Window.** Cut a 2x4 sill to fit between the studs on each side of the window. Position the sill 1/2 inch below the window. This allows room for drywall on the sill. If

Chalk line

**4** Raise the framework into position, and align it with the layout chalk lines on the floor (top). Plumb the wall, and drive shims between the top plate and the joists to lock the structure into place (bottom). Then nail through the plate and the shims into the joists.

Chalk line

**5** Align the bottom of the framework with the chalk line, then nail through the plate into the floor.

Sill

Cripple Stud

**6** Cut a sill to fit between studs, and then nail it into place beneath the window. Add framing as needed to fill in beneath the window plate, and toenail it to the bottom plate.

**7** When installing foil-faced fiberglass batts, staple their flanges to the studs. Do not leave gaps.

there is masonry over the window, you'll also need a header block, set 1/2 inch above the window. Fill in framing beneath the lower block as needed to maintain 16-inch on-center spacing along the wall. To let more light into the basement, angle the drywall away from the window and reposition the sill accordingly. (See page 48 for another way to frame around windows.)

**7** **Installing the Insulation.** The secondary walls must have a vapor barrier on the warm side of the studs. It prevents moist air from flowing through the framework and condensing on the cooler surface of the masonry walls. One way to provide the vapor barrier is to insulate with foil-faced fiberglass batts. Staple the flanges of insulation to the studs, and eliminate all gaps.

***Caution:*** *When working with insulation protect yourself from the fibers that inevitably are released into the air. Wear a dust mask, eye protection, a long-sleeve shirt, a hat, gloves, and long pants during the installation and whenever insulation is cut or moved.*

When using fiberglass batts, do not to leave areas of the wall, including the rim joist, uninsulated. Insulate behind all plumbing pipes; they must be located on the warm side of the insulation. Partition walls between heated rooms need not be insulated.

At this point, the framework is ready for drywall or paneling.

## *Installing Rigid Insulation*

Instead of building secondary walls solely for the purpose of holding fiberglass insulation, an option is to apply rigid insulation directly to foundation walls. This product, which has insulation values that range from R-4 to R-7 per inch, is made from a variety of plastic materials, including expanded polystyrene, extruded polystyrene, polyurethane and polyisocyanurate. All of the products come in easy-to-handle sheets and some are designed specifically for insulating foundation walls. Some products (at least one brand of extruded polystyrene) have rabbeted edges that can be held in place with 1x3 wood cleats. Although extruded polystyrene is very resistant

to moisture, the foundation walls must be dry before they can be insulated. (See page 20.)

The following system features extruded polystyrene that is rabbeted on the edges and held in place with wood cleats. The insulation itself is 1½ inches thick and has an R-value of 7.5. Sheets are 2x8 feet so the cleats are installed on 24-inch centers. Drywall also is nailed on 2-foot centers instead of the more typical 16-inch centers. Installing them this way works because the drywall is fully supported by cleats and insulation. Check with local code officials, however, to make sure this method is permitted in your area.

**1** **Cutting Sheets.** Measure for the cut and mark it by scoring the insulation lightly with the tip of a nail. Use a utility knife to cut part way through the sheet and break the piece off over the edge of a work surface. Use this method to cut each panel so it fits exactly between floor and wall. Cut 1x3 wood cleats to the same height as the insulation.

**2** **Placing Sheets.** Start at one corner of the wall. Hold a sheet of insulation against the wall (trim one edge, if necessary, to fit into an out-of-plumb corner) and plumb it. This

**1** Use a utility knife guided by a metal straightedge to cut insulation. Support the insulation fully on a worktable, then snap it along the cut. It is not necessary to cut all the way through the material.

**2** Start at one corner of the wall. Hold a panel against the wall and plumb it. The panel must fit tightly in the corner.

**3** Drill through the cleat and into the foundation. Then use concrete screws to secure the cleat. Make sure the head of each screw is flush with the surface of the cleat.

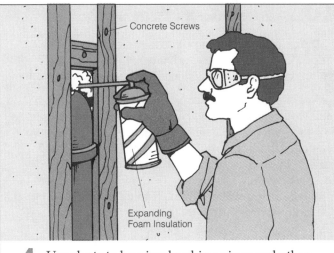

Concrete Screws

Expanding Foam Insulation

**4** Use cleats to box-in plumbing pipes and other obstructions. Use expanding foam sealant to fill gaps. Wear gloves and eye protection when using this product. Do not overfill gaps.

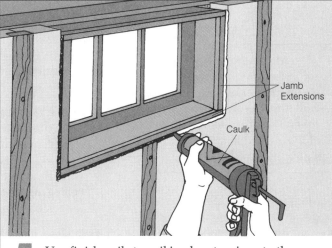

Jamb Extensions

Caulk

**5** Use finish nails to nail jamb extensions to the edges of windows and doors. Butt insulation to the extensions and use caulk to seal gaps between them.

first sheet determines how plumb adjacent sheets will be so make sure it is done right.

**3** **Installing Cleats.** Hold a second sheet against the first and slip a 1x3 wood cleat into the channel between them. Drill three or four pilot holes through the cleat and into the foundation. Pull away the cleat and deepen the holes as needed. Then clear debris from the holes and use concrete screws to secure the cleat. Continue working along the wall in this fashion. Periodically check the insulation for plumb.

**4** **Working Around Obstructions.** If small pipes or other obstructions cannot be moved, work around them by placing cleats on either side. Odd-shaped spaces can be filled with expanding spray foam but it must be a type that is compatible with the insulation. Continue laying out the sheets; make sure the cleats maintain the 24-inch on-center spacing.

**5** **Sealing the Edges.** Cut jamb extensions to a size equaling the combined thickness of insulation and drywall and nail them to window and door jambs. (Jamb extensions

are slender pieces of wood that are nailed to the jambs with finishing nails. They are used to extend the jambs so that they are flush with the finished surface of the adjoining wall.) Use a table saw to cut jamb extensions from 3/4-inch-thick stock. Once the extensions are attached use latex caulk to seal small gaps where the insulation meets window or door framing.

**6** **Detailing the Corners.** A solid support must be provided for the edge of each drywall sheet, particularly at corners. At inside

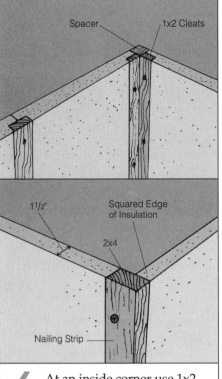

Spacer    1x2 Cleats

1½"    Squared Edge of Insulation

2x4

Nailing Strip

**6** At an inside corner use 1x2 cleats and a wood spacer to ensure proper nailing for the drywall (top). At an outside corner, rip nailing strips to the thickness of the insulation and screw one side to the wall (bottom).

corners place two cleats edge to edge with a square strip of wood in the corner between them. For outside corners, rip nailing strips to fit the corner. In this case, the strip has to be at least 1½ inches thick and 3 inches wide, so a 2 x 4 is a good fit. Screw the strip into the corner.

**7** **Installing the Drywall.** When the insulation is in place, the drywall is installed and finished in the usual way (see page 69) except that the nailing is done on 24-inch centers instead of 16-inch centers. This spacing works because the insulation provides a firm backing for the drywall rather than a partial backing that is common to a framed wall. Code requires that all areas of rigid insulation that face a living space must be covered, usually by drywall. This is because rigid insulation is combustible; leaving it exposed in living areas poses a fire hazard.

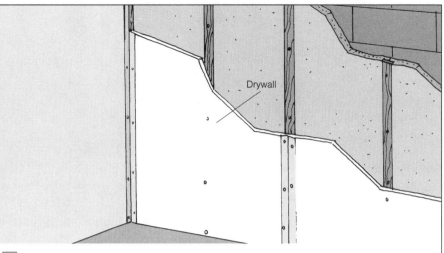

Drywall

**7** Using standard drywall nails or screws and standard spacing, attach the drywall to the wood cleats and nailing strips.

## Optional Insulation Method

This method of installing rigid insulation provides the chance to use a greater variety of rigid insulation sheets and allows for a variety of insulation thicknesses. It does not, however, result in an unbroken insulating layer.

First screw or nail 1x2 wood nailers, called furring strips, to the walls. Then fit sheets of 3/4-inch-thick rigid insulation between them and staple a plastic vapor barrier over the assembly. A dab of compatible adhesive caulking holds the sheets in place until the assembly is covered with drywall. Be sure that the foundation walls are free from moisture problems before insulation is installed. Drywall or 1/4-inch-thick wood paneling (or thicker) can be nailed or screwed directly to the furring strips.

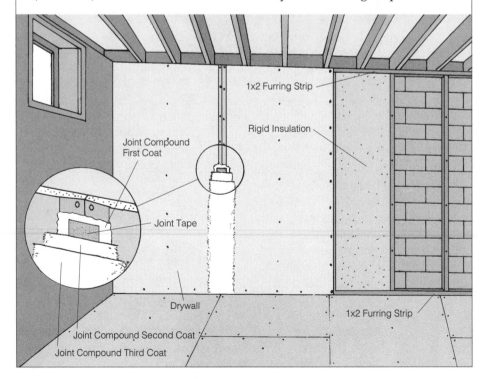

1x2 Furring Strip

Rigid Insulation

Joint Compound First Coat

Joint Tape

Drywall

1x2 Furring Strip

Joint Compound Second Coat

Joint Compound Third Coat

# WINDOWS & DOORS

When it comes to basement windows, the key is to make the most of what you have. First, repair or replace damaged windows. Then trim the windows to fit the decor of the new room. Be aware that building codes require special windows for some basement rooms.

# Windows

Unless yours is a daylight basement (a basement with at least one wall exposed to the grade), it probably does not have much by way of windows. For a recreation room or a home office this is not a problem—simply wire the room so that it has plenty of artificial light. When it comes to bedrooms, however, building codes come into play.

## Building Codes & Basement Windows

Whether or not a window has to be added to a basement is not entirely a matter of personal preference. All bedrooms, including those in a basement, require a means of emergency exit.

If there is a door that leads directly outside (and not to a bulkhead door; see page 52), it can be considered an emergency exit. If there is no door, however, each *bedroom* must have at least one egress window. The requirements for such a window specify its minimum size, its "net clear opening," and the maximum distance between the sill and floor. The net clear opening essentially is the square footage of space available for a person to climb through once the window is fully open. It is

measured between obstructions, such as window stops, that obstruct passage. The minimum net clear opening for bedroom egress windows is 5 square feet.

## Replacing a Wood Window

One problem with wood-framed basement windows is that they are susceptible to rot and insect damage. In some cases the affected wood simply can be cut away and repaired with epoxy wood filler, but extensive damage calls for replacement of the entire window. Measure the size of the rough opening (the hole in the wall in which the window sits) and check local window sources to see if replacement windows are readily available. If not, a custom-built window has to be ordered. This may take some time so do not remove the old window until the new one is on hand. Replacement methods vary depending on how the original window was installed so pay attention as the old one is removed.

## Window Details

If the inside of the foundation is to be insulated, the window frames must be "boxed-out" to match the combined thickness of insulation and finished wall surfaces. Given the variety of window sizes, frame types and locations, there is no one best way to do

this. If the window is an egress window, however, check with local building officials before proceeding—boxing-out a window sometimes affects its accessibility. The following are some options to consider:

**Secondary Wall Framing.** For wood-framed walls that are built to insulate the foundation, there are several ways to finish the area around foundation windows. The simplest way is to treat the window as if it were in a standard frame wall. A 2x4 sill nailed between studs forms the rough opening, while the ceiling butts into the top of the window. The new jambs and sill may be finished with paneling or drywall. Remember to consider their thickness when the framing is installed. (See page 41.)

An alternative to boxing-out a recess is to bevel the windowsill. This takes planning and some carpentry skills, but results in a brighter basement because the light is reflected into the room rather than blocked off.

**1** **Framing the Wall.** In order to provide clearance for the beveled windowsill, the framing immediately beneath the window has to be shorter than it would be otherwise. For a 45-degree bevel, the framework must be shorter by the width of the studs (3½ inches, for example, if

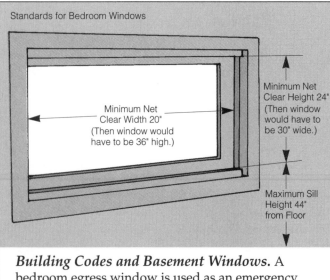

***Building Codes and Basement Windows.*** A bedroom egress window is used as an emergency exit. The net clear opening cannot be less than 5 sq. ft.

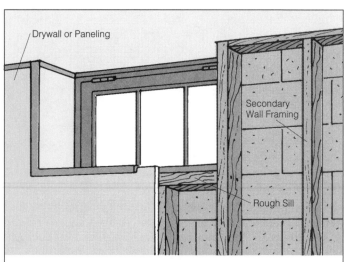

***Secondary Wall Framing.*** In places where a secondary wall meets a window, the framing can be detailed to support finished wall surfaces.

framing with 2x4 lumber). For a steeper bevel, the framework must be shorter. Frame the wall, tip it into place and fasten it to the floor and the underside of the joists. (See page 38.)

**2** **Installing the Blocking.** Cut 1x4 blocking to the width of the window and attach it to the foundation with concrete screws. (Avoid masonry nails when working this close to the edge of the masonry.) Cut a 45-degree bevel on a length of

1-by or 2-by stock that is the same length as the first piece, and nail it to the top of the framed wall. (It provides support for the sill panel.) The top edge of the blocking can be beveled as well, if desired.

**3** **Installing the Sill Panel.** The sill panel can be plywood, drywall, or even paneling to match surrounding paneling. In any case, cut a piece to fit beneath the window, and tack it temporarily in place. (It may have to

be trimmed slightly after the finished wall surfaces have been installed.)

**4** **Trimming out the Bevel.** After the finished wall surfaces are installed (usually drywall or plywood paneling), trim the sill panel as necessary for a good fit. Put insulation behind the panel, and then nail it to the support and the blocking underneath. Add a sill to cap the top of the panel. Use corner bead or wood trim to cap the bottom.

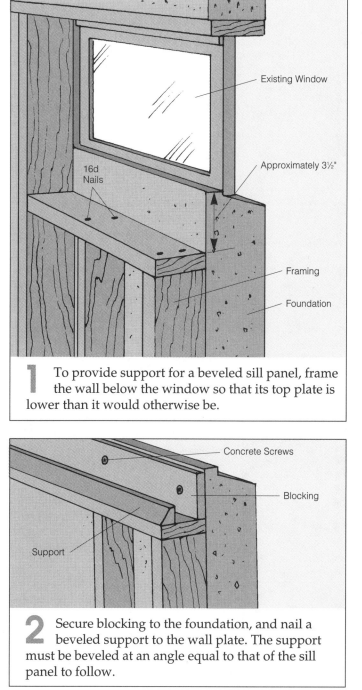

**1** To provide support for a beveled sill panel, frame the wall below the window so that its top plate is lower than it would otherwise be.

**2** Secure blocking to the foundation, and nail a beveled support to the wall plate. The support must be beveled at an angle equal to that of the sill panel to follow.

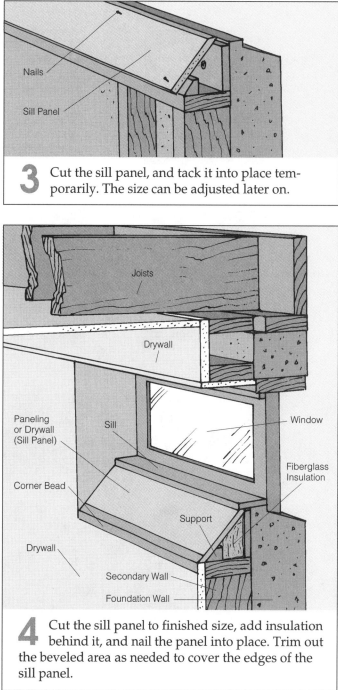

**3** Cut the sill panel, and tack it into place temporarily. The size can be adjusted later on.

**4** Cut the sill panel to finished size, add insulation behind it, and nail the panel into place. Trim out the beveled area as needed to cover the edges of the sill panel.

## Window Trim

After the window is boxed consider the finishing touches. Small windows generally look best with simple frames of mitered casing without a window stool or apron (called "picture frame" trim). For large basement windows, many types of casing details are possible, nearly all of which use some version of the two basic joints: the miter joint and the butt joint. A miter joint occurs in places where two pieces of wood are joined at an angle (typically 90 degrees). This joint often is used in places, such as a corner, where trim changes direction. A butt joint is the simplest joint of all. Both of the mating pieces are cut square and one is simply "butted" into the other. This joint often is used in places where trim pieces that have different thickness or shapes meet.

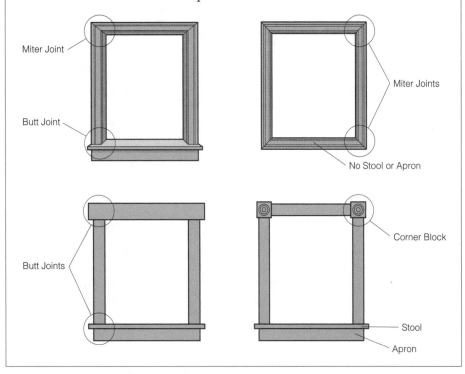

1 Dig a hole that is big enough to contain the window well. Allow several inches of leeway to maneuver the well into position.

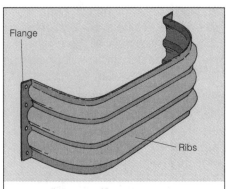

***Window Wells.*** Choose one that is 6 in. wider than the window opening and deep enough to extend 8 in. below the level of the windowsill.

## Window Wells

It is possible to fit a small window at the top of a foundation wall and still maintain the mandatory 6 inches above grade (the code minimum). This code is intended to protect wood building elements from rot by keeping soil away from them. If the windows are too close to the soil try to lower the nearby grade level (make sure it still slopes away from the foundation). The soil that is removed probably can be used elsewhere in yard. If the grade cannot be lowered, a window well has to be installed.

A window well works like a dam to hold soil away from a window that is located partially below grade. Though a well can be built with concrete block, many people find it easier to use a galvanized steel product purchased from a home center. The ribs in a well give it strength, and flanges at each end allow it to be bolted to the foundation walls. Wells come in various sizes. Choose one that is at least 6 inches wider than the window opening and deep enough to extend at least 8 inches below the level of the windowsill.

1 **Digging the Hole.** Place the well next to the house and use it as a template to mark the perimeter of the hole. Do not try to dig a precise hole. Allow several inches of leeway to maneuver the well into position. Then wash dirt off the newly exposed por-

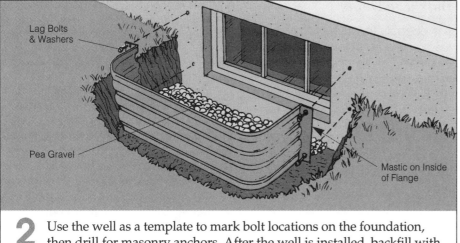

Lag Bolts & Washers

Pea Gravel

Mastic on Inside of Flange

**2** Use the well as a template to mark bolt locations on the foundation, then drill for masonry anchors. After the well is installed, backfill with pea gravel and place a layer of gravel in the bottom for drainage purposes.

tions of the foundation. To allow room for gravel dig 4 or 5 inches deeper than the depth of the well. (Remember, the top of the well must be approximately 6 inches above grade.)

**2** **Attaching the Well.** Hold the well against the foundation and mark the position of the mounting holes. Drill the foundation to accept masonry fasteners. (See page 36.) Coat the contact areas with asphalt

mastic and install the well. Backfill with pea gravel, then shovel 4 or 5 inches of pea gravel into the well itself (to improve drainage). To keep out accumulations of snow and debris, cover the well with a clear plastic cover.

## Doors & Door Framing

The framing around doors in a basement is fairly simple because the

partitions are not load bearing. Thus, there is no need for a structural header above the door. Many do-it-yourselfers find prehung doors easiest to install. (They can be installed whether or not a structural header is in place.) These factory-assembled units eliminate some rather fussy carpentry work. Because the size of the rough opening depends on the size of the door and its frame, it is best to purchase the door before the wall is framed. It generally is easiest to install the door after the drywall has been installed.

**1** **Framing the Rough Opening.** Since none of the walls are load bearing, simple door framing is appropriate. The framing for the rough opening of the door can be installed before the wall is tipped into place. The rough opening generally is 1/2 inch wider and 1/4 inch taller than the outside dimensions of the door jambs. This allows room to shim the unit so that it is plumb and level.

**2** **Installing the Jambs.** Remove all nails that secure the door to the jambs, then set the unit in the

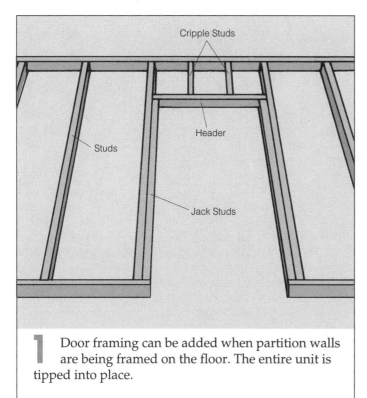

Cripple Studs

Header

Studs

Jack Studs

**1** Door framing can be added when partition walls are being framed on the floor. The entire unit is tipped into place.

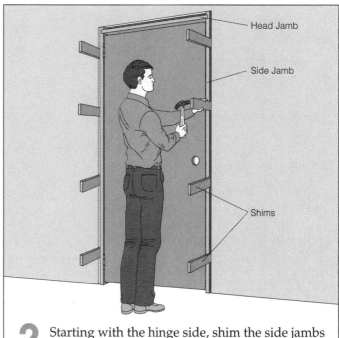

Head Jamb

Side Jamb

Shims

**2** Starting with the hinge side, shim the side jambs of the door. The wedge-shaped shims are inserted in pairs from opposite sides of the wall. Use 8d casing or finish nails to nail through the shims as they are installed.

rough opening. Using the door itself as a guide, install wood shims to adjust the position of the jambs in the opening. Start by shimming between the floor and the side jambs as needed to level the head jamb (these shims are only temporary; remove them when the jambs are nailed in place). Then shim the jamb that has the hinges on it so that it is straight and plumb (a 4-foot level is ideal for this but not required). Finally, shim the opposite jamb.

**3** **Checking Clearances.** Start at the top when shimming the jamb on the strike side of the door. Try to maintain the existing distance between door and jamb all the way down the jamb. Open the door periodically to make sure it swings properly.

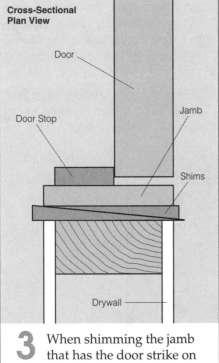

**Cross-Sectional Plan View**

Door

Door Stop

Jamb

Shims

Drywall

**3** When shimming the jamb that has the door strike on it, maintain an even clearance between door and jamb over the entire length of the jamb.

## Bulkhead Doors

It is possible to have a door that leads to the outside of the house, even in a basement that is completely below grade. Such a door can provide an emergency exit, although it does not qualify as a bedroom egress under the code. A bulkhead door also provides convenience. It is easier to get furniture into the basement if it does not have to be lugged through the house. If the basement is going to be used as a shop, a door is essential for getting plywood, lumber, and large tools inside.

Adding a door is a big job—it involves cutting a large hole in the

foundation and pouring concrete retaining walls to hold back the earth—a job best left to the professionals. An exterior passage door is framed into the new opening in the foundation. A retaining wall supports concrete or steel stairs which lead up to a bulkhead door. A bulkhead door typically is made of steel and has two outwardly swinging panels that can be opened from the inside. It caps the stairwell and keeps out rain, snow and debris. The passage door at the bottom of the stairway should be an exterior-grade, insulated metal door with a metal frame. The insulated metal won't rot and keeps cold air from seeping into the basement.

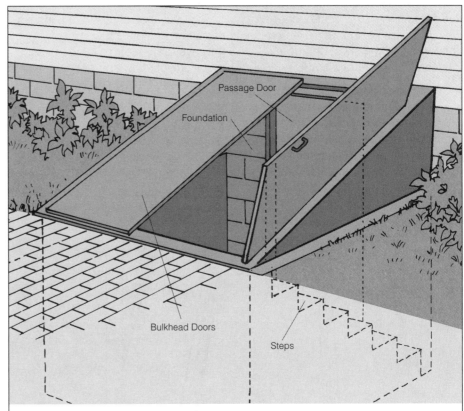

Passage Door

Foundation

Bulkhead Doors

Steps

**Bulkhead Doors.** The steel panels of the bulkhead door protect the stairwell from weather. An insulated metal passage door keeps heat in the basement.

# WIRING & PLUMBING

It is essential to have an electrical plan that anticipates your needs. Luckily, wiring is relatively easy for a do-it-yourselfer to plan and install. Adding plumbing is a tougher task, but may be worth the effort and expense if a new bathroom makes the basement more livable.

# Wiring

Once some of the basic concepts are understood, wiring is not difficult. It does, however, require attention to safety and stringent adherence to electrical codes. In some parts of the country only licensed electricians can work on household wiring, while in other locales a homeowner may work on every part of his or her own house. Be sure to check local codes before beginning a wiring project.

Building codes require that the basement be supplied by at least one circuit, though at least one additional circuit will make the basement far more convenient to use. A home office has considerable electrical requirements so plan at least one circuit for this room alone.

## Tools for Wiring

If framing is exposed for "rough" wiring work (running wires and installing boxes), the only tools needed are a hammer, wire cutter, and an electric drill with a 5/8-inch auger or

spade bit (for drilling through the studs). The "finished" wiring work requires a small collection of hand tools (detailed in the following list). Electrical tape is needed as well.

**Fish Tape.** This tool essentially is a roll of stiff wire that has a hook on one end to which wire cable is attached. It is used to pull wire through the wall. Fish tape is not

needed unless the basement was finished partially at an earlier date and is now getting expanded.

**Needle-nose Pliers.** This is the perfect tool for snipping a wire to length and then bending the end into a tight loop to go around terminal screws.

**Wire Strippers.** The cutter holes on this tool match diameters of various wire gauges and easily strip insula-

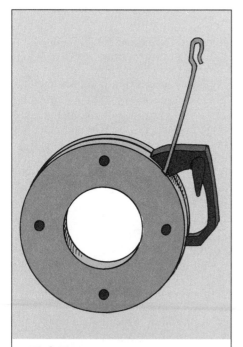

*Fish Tape.* This resilient metal wire is used to pull electrical cable through otherwise inaccessible places.

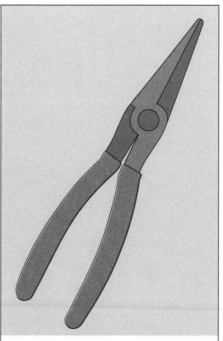

*Needle-nose Pliers.* This convenient tool is used to snip wire and bend it into a tight loop.

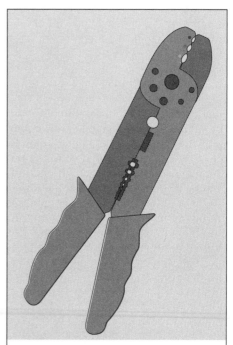

*Wire Strippers.* This tool has cutter holes with diameters to match various wire gauges. It easily strips off insulation without nicking the wire itself.

tion off the wire without nicking the wire itself.

**Screwdrivers.** A standard slot screwdriver and a Phillips screwdriver are needed.

**Voltage Tester.** With probes inserted, this inexpensive tool is used to test for the presence of electricity.

**Service Entrance Panel.** Electricity enters the house through a meter that measures the amount of electricity used. Then it flows into the service entrance panel. The panel essentially is a distribution center. It divides incoming electricity into branch circuits that serve various portions of the house. Each circuit is protected by a fuse (in older panels) or a circuit breaker (in newer panels) that cuts power to a circuit in the event of an overload or circuit fault. Each circuit is independent of the others, so when power is cut to one, the remaining circuits are unaffected and continue to supply power.

The job of adding circuits to supply the basement consists of cutting power to the service panel, adding one or more circuit breakers, running wires throughout the basement, and connecting all the outlets and switches to the new circuit. Those who are not familiar with this work are advised to turn it over to a licensed electrician. One cost-saving option, however, is to do the time-consuming work of routing the wiring while leaving all connections to the electrician. Before doing so, however, find an electrician who is willing to work this way.

## Running Wires

House circuits usually are wired with nonmetallic sheathed cable (often referred to by the trade name Romex). Nonmetallic cable is flexible and easier to work with than other types of cable. A cable contains two or more copper wires within a protective plastic sheathing and is sold by the foot or in rolls of 25, 50, or 100 feet. Aluminum wire was used widely from World War II until the mid-1970s but is no longer considered suitable for

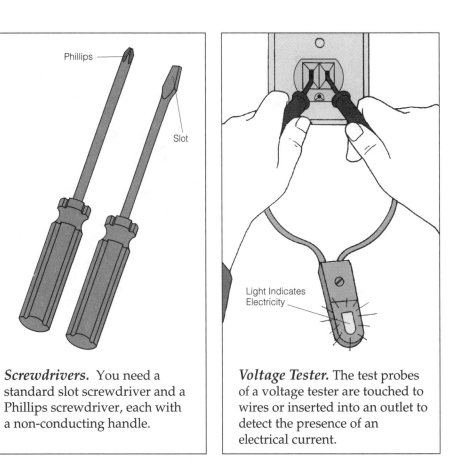

*Screwdrivers.* You need a standard slot screwdriver and a Phillips screwdriver, each with a non-conducting handle.

*Voltage Tester.* The test probes of a voltage tester are touched to wires or inserted into an outlet to detect the presence of an electrical current.

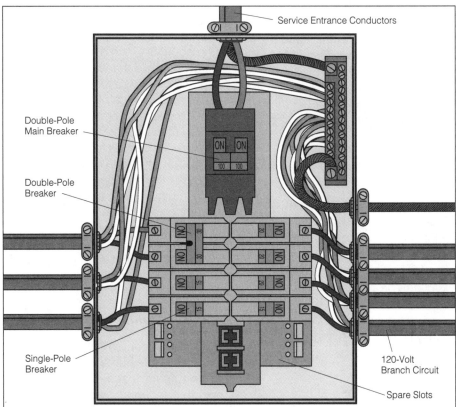

*Service Entrance Panel.* Each incoming cable is connected to a separate circuit breaker. The panel shown here has room for four additional breakers which means it can serve as many as four new basement circuits.

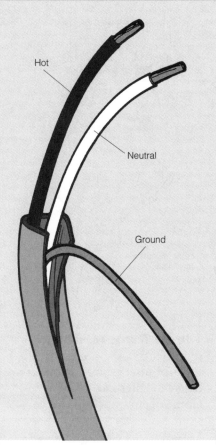

***Running Wires.*** Nonmetallic sheathed cable is the standard cable used in residential wiring. Its outer sheathing, made of flexible plastic, protects several individual wires inside.

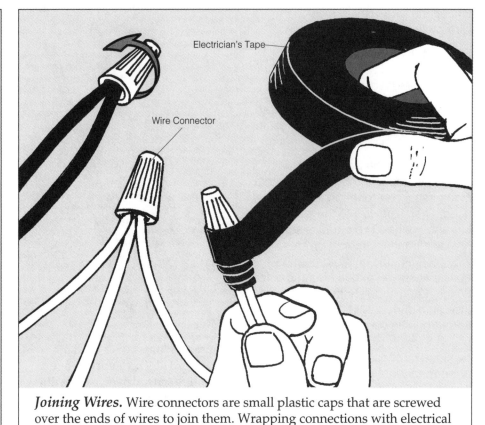

***Joining Wires.*** Wire connectors are small plastic caps that are screwed over the ends of wires to join them. Wrapping connections with electrical tape is a good idea, although not required by the National Electrical Code.

household wiring. Consult an electrician before modifying an aluminum wire system in any way.

Wiring that loops through the house is supported by cable staples. A hammer is used to drive these heavy-duty staples into the framing lumber. One box of staples is enough for most basement projects. Make sure the staples are a suitable size in relation to the wire being used (this information usually is found on the staple box).

## Joining Wires

At one time all wires in a household system were spliced together with solder and electrical tape. Now splices are made by joining wires with plastic caps called wire connectors. The inner portion of each cap is threaded. To join two or more wires, strip about 3/4 inch of insulation from each wire, hold the wires together and in a clockwise motion, twist on the wire connector. (There is no need to twist the wires together first, though many people do.) Simply unscrew the connector to remove it. Connectors come in many sizes; choosing the right one depends on the number of wires to be joined and the gauge of the wires. Usually, however, a connector is used to join two or three No. 14 or No. 12 wires. For most basement wiring projects, it is cost-effective to buy a box of wire connectors in the size needed most.

## Types of Cable

The individual wires (called conductors) in a cable come in a range of sizes. Circuits that serve lighting and standard receptacles, however, typically are No. 14 wire diameter (rated to carry a maximum of 15 amps) or No. 12 wire diameter (rated to carry a maximum of 20 amps). Amperage is a measure of current flow. Markings on the plastic sheathing of cable explain what is inside and identify the type of insulation that covers it. For example, consider the following designation:

14/2 WITH GROUND, TYPE NM, 600V (UL)

The number before the slash mark indicates the size of the wire inside the cable (No. 14). The number after indicates how many conductors (two in this case) are in the cable. There also is an equipment grounding wire, as indicated. (The ground wire is not considered a conductor.) In this case, the type designation indicates a cable that is for use only in dry locations (indoors). Each wire is wrapped in its own plastic insulating sheath, though the ground wire may be bare. Following the type is a number that indicates the maximum voltage allowed through the cable. Finally, the UL (Underwriters Laboratories) notation specifies that the cable has been certified as safe for the uses for which it was designed. For safety reasons, never use wiring or other electrical supplies that do not bear the UL notation.

## Estimating Wire Needs

New wiring that leads from the service panel to the first switch or outlet in the basement must be of a continuous, unbroken length. The code allows certain exceptions to this, but a single length is ideal and nearly always possible. Wiring may have to be snaked over, around, or through a number of obstructions as it is routed through the basement. Rather than try to calculate the length of this path, simply begin with a 25-foot roll of wiring. In most cases this is more than enough and the excess can be used for general wiring in the basement.

When running wire through a structure in which all the walls and new partitions are exposed, it is fairly easy to figure out the amount of wire needed. Measure the distance between each connection to be made, add a foot for every connection and then add 20 percent to the total to provide a margin of error.

## Wiring Framed Walls

Running wire from the service panel through the basement usually is easier than running it to other parts of the house. Every house calls for a different strategy but the following guide provides some techniques for solving typical problems. Wires are not connected to a power source until they have been safely connected to outlets or fixtures.

**1 Wiring at the Panel.** Start the run with a 4-foot tail of wire at the service panel. This allows enough wire for the electrician to connect the circuit breaker.

**2 Securing Cable.** Use cable staples to support the cable at 4-foot intervals (or according to local code). Do not damage the outer casing of the wire as the staple is driven home. Support the cable on both sides of a corner.

**3 Drilling Through Framing.** In places where cable passes through framing, drill a 3/4-inch-diameter hole to allow room to pull the wiring. Though a spade bit can be used, an auger bit is easier and safer. Auger bits are available at

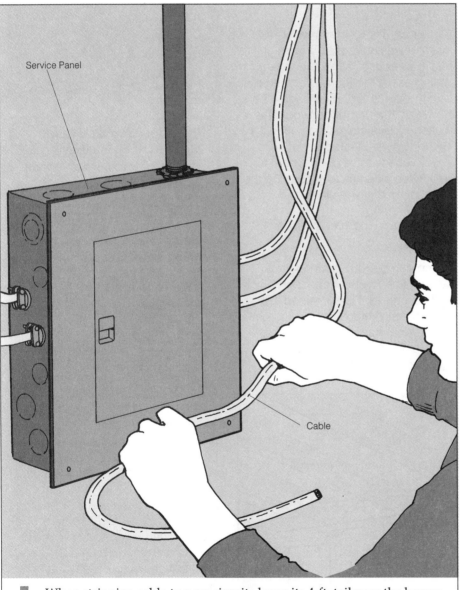

**1** When stringing cable to new circuits leave its 4-ft. tail near the box so the electrician can connect it to the proper circuit breaker.

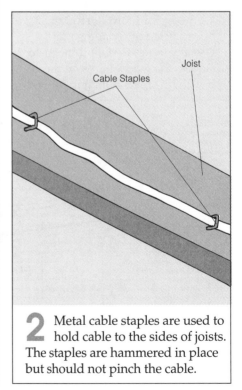

**2** Metal cable staples are used to hold cable to the sides of joists. The staples are hammered in place but should not pinch the cable.

many hardware and home supply stores. When drilling through framing, the hole must be at least 1¼ inch away from the edge of the stud or joist to minimize the risk that a paneling or drywall nail will hit the wire. If the hole is closer than 1¼ inch, the National Electrical Code requires that the wiring be protected with a

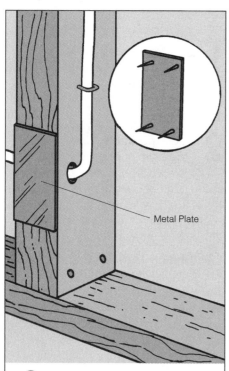

**3** Cable that passes close to the edge of a joist or stud must be protected by a nailing plate. Use a hammer to pound the plate against the wood; barbs on the back of the plate hold it in place.

metal plate. (Plates are available at many hardware stores and other places where electrical supplies are sold.)

**4 Drilling Through Joists.** Use the same bit used for drilling through studs to drill through joists. Always put the hole in the center one-third of the board. (The joist is weakened when drilled through the bottom third and nails may get in the way if it is placed in the upper third.)

## Wiring in Masonry Walls

Since it is difficult to run wiring and install boxes on masonry walls, it may be easier to build secondary walls against the foundation and run wire through them. (See page 42.) However, if wiring directly onto the masonry walls makes sense read the following step-by-step project. Be sure to check local codes, particularly when it comes to grounding the metal parts of the system.

### Installing Surface-Mount Systems

Wiring can be routed along the surface of a concrete or concrete block wall as long as it is contained in a system that protects the wires from mechanical damage. One system calls for the use of metal boxes and thin-wall metal conduit called EMT.

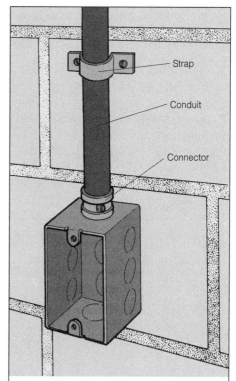

***Installing Surface-Mount Systems.*** Individual conductors are routed through lightweight metal tubing that is connected to each electrical box.

Special connectors form a tight seal between box and conduit. Conduit is secured with metal straps that are screwed to the masonry. Electrical boxes also are screwed in place. Installing the system calls for special tools, and because sheathed cable is too bulky, individual wires have to be pulled through the conduit.

A similar surface-mount system is easier for do-it-yourselfers to install. Instead of metal conduit, it uses plastic track with a snap-on cover to contain the wire, along with a series of fittings for changing direction and splicing lengths of track together. (Check local codes before installing this kind of system.) The only special tools needed are a hacksaw and an electric drill and carbide bits. The system itself can be purchased at home center stores. Make a sketch of the basement that shows approximately where switches, outlets, and fixture boxes will be installed and bring it shopping with you. If the supplier

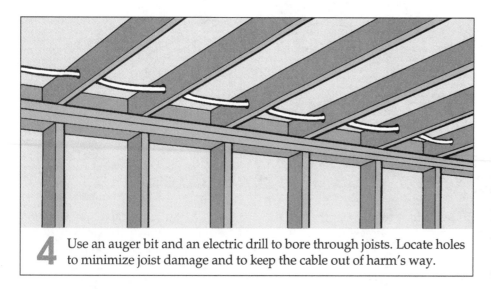

**4** Use an auger bit and an electric drill to bore through joists. Locate holes to minimize joist damage and to keep the cable out of harm's way.

allows unused materials to be returned, purchase more supplies than you think are necessary.

## 1 Installing the Power Feed.
Surface-mount systems utilize single conductors rather than sheathed cable. Sheathed cable, however, can be used to connect the surface-mount system to the service panel. A special adapter plate that fits over a standard electrical box makes the transition from sheathed cable to individual conductors. The surface-mount box contains cutouts in all four sides of the box to accommodate track that goes up, down, or to the side.

## 2 Installing Channels and Elbows.
Begin at the starter box and install lengths of base track (available in 5-foot lengths). Drill a hole through the base track every 18 inches and 1/2 inch from each end. Then use it as a template for marking holes on the wall. Drill holes in the wall for concrete screws or plastic shields, then screw the base track to the wall. (Be careful not to tighten screws so much that they damage the track.) Route the base track to the area of each switch and outlet box and secure the box with concrete screws or plastic shields according the manufacturer's instructions.

## 3 Installing Intersections.
In the places where lengths of base track intersect mid-run, cut away the lip of the track to make room for wires. Tracks that intersect at an inside or outside corner are butted together. Turns on the same wall are mitered. Use a hacksaw and a miter box to make the cuts.

## 4 Running Wires.
Surface-mount systems use type THHN conductors instead of sheathed cable. As many as ten 14-gauge conductors can fit in a channel. (Only seven 12-gauge conductors fit.) Use plastic clips to hold wires that stretch from switches to boxes.

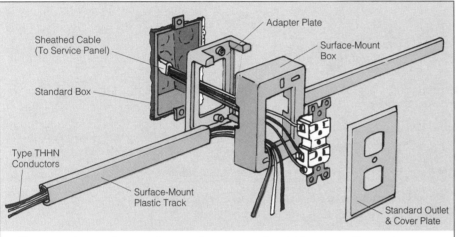

**1** Attach an adapter plate to the existing box. Then install a surface-mount box and connect the surface-mount track to it.

**2** Drill holes in the base track. Use the track as a template for marking holes in the masonry.

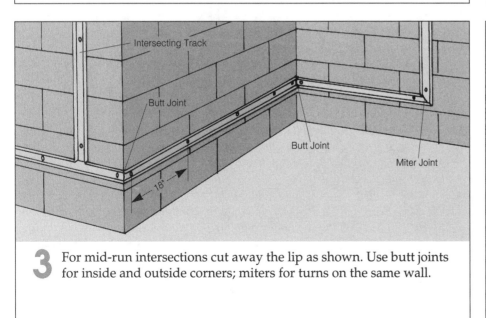

**3** For mid-run intersections cut away the lip as shown. Use butt joints for inside and outside corners; miters for turns on the same wall.

**4** Route individual conductors to each switch, outlet and fixture served by the surface-mount track.

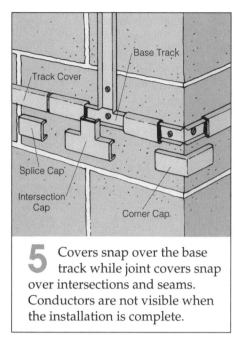

Base Track

Track Cover

Splice Cap

Intersection Cap

Corner Cap

**5** Covers snap over the base track while joint covers snap over intersections and seams. Conductors are not visible when the installation is complete.

**5** **Capping the Base Track.** Cut lengths of base-track cover to fit over the base track and snap them in place. Cut covers 1⅜ inches short of each intersection to accommodate the various joint covers.

### Relocating Existing Wiring

In most cases, a great deal of wiring already exists in the basement. These wires feed circuits elsewhere in the house and may have to be moved depending on where they are and what is planned for the basement ceiling.

If wires run through holes in the joists, there is no need to worry about them unless they come closer than 1¼ inch to the edge of a joist. If so, nail a protective metal plate to the joist to prevent the wires from being punctured by nails. If a suspended ceiling is to be installed, the wires do not have to be relocated. (See page 73.) However, if a drywall ceiling will be installed and wires run along the underside of the joists, the wires must be relocated.

**1** **Loosening the Wires.** Use nippers to grasp the edge of each cable staple, then lever out the staple. As this is done do not crush the cable beneath the nippers and do not nick the outer casing of the

cable. Move the wires aside temporarily and dispose of the staples.

**2** **Cutting a Notch.** According to building codes, notches in the bottom of a joist must be no more than 1/6 the depth of the joist, and they must not be located in the middle third of a joist's length. If these

criteria cannot be met disconnect the circuit and run the wires through holes in the joists. To lay out the notch, set an adjustable square to the depth of the notch (making the notch just deep enough to contain the wires), and mark cut lines on the edge of each joist. Use a saber saw or handsaw to cut both sides of the notch.

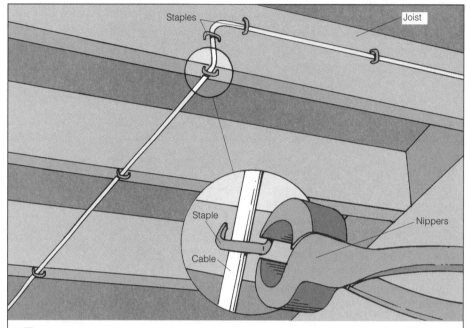

Staples

Joist

Staple

Cable

Nippers

**1** To remove a cable staple, grasp one side with nippers and pull out the staple. Do not damage the cable itself.

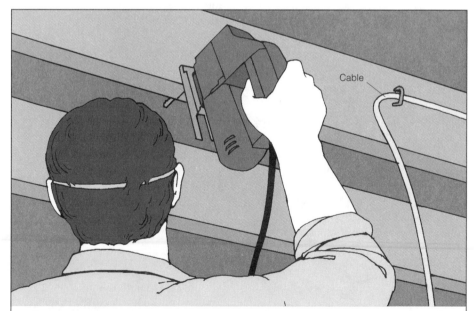

Cable

**2** Never notch a joist in the middle third of its length. Mark cut lines for notches where cable crosses each joist and use a saber saw or handsaw to make the shallow cuts.

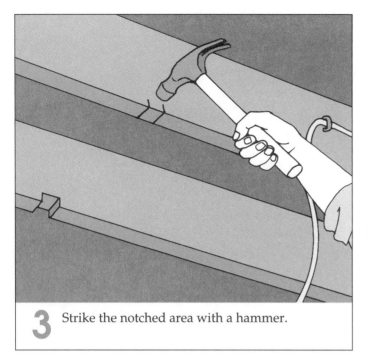

**3** Strike the notched area with a hammer.

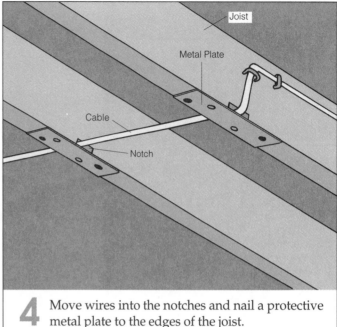

**4** Move wires into the notches and nail a protective metal plate to the edges of the joist.

**3 Completing the Notch.** The bottom of the notch will be parallel to the grain of the joist so the waste wood can be knocked out easily by striking it with a hammer. If necessary, use a chisel to clean up the bottom of the notch.

**4 Relocating the Wires.** Move wires into the notch. (If necessary, use a cable staple to hold them.) According to electrical codes, the wires must be protected by a metal plate that is at least 1/16 inch thick.

# Plumbing

For those who have basic skills in cutting and soldering copper pipe, the job of adding piping to supply water to a basement sink or toilet is straightforward. Providing a drain and vent for the water, however, remains a difficult job. The following information is meant to provide do-it-yourselfers with an idea of what is involved in such a project. This is a job, however, for a professional. Especially if the basement is below the level of the existing DWV (drain/waste/vent) system. (Usually it is.) Contact a plumber before finalizing a room arrangement in the basement. He or she probably will suggest a placement or fixtures that minimize effort and expense.

**Adding New Supply Lines.** The hot and cold water supplied to fixtures throughout the house runs through copper or (in older houses) galvanized-steel pipes. New pipes are nearly always copper. The water in a household supply system is under pressure so pipes can run at all angles. This makes it easy to supply the basement with water. After turning off the water at the main, draining the water to the lowest fixture, and tapping into an existing line, simply solder lengths of copper pipe together until the fixture is reached. The lines to each fixture terminate in a shutoff valve. When adding supply lines, run piping parallel to the floor joists wherever possible, and tuck it into the space between joists.

## Relocating Existing Supply Lines

Pipes that supply water to fixtures upstairs often are attached to the underside of the floor joists. If a drywall ceiling is to be installed in the basement, the pipes have to be relocated. This can be done if there are not many pipes to move. (However, if the house has hot-water or steam radiators, there will be too many pipes to move. Consider a suspended ceiling instead.) The existing pipes may be reused or it may be easier to replace the old pipe with new pipe.

**1 Marking the Runs.** Run a carpenter's pencil or a marker along the sides of the existing horizontal pipes to mark the underside of the joists for notches. The pipes most commonly encountered are 1/2 inch, 3/4 inch or 1 inch. (These are internal measurements.) The outside of a

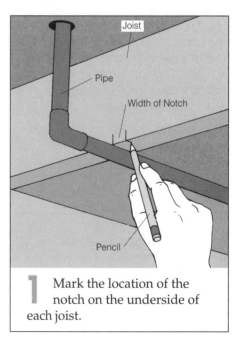

**1** Mark the location of the notch on the underside of each joist.

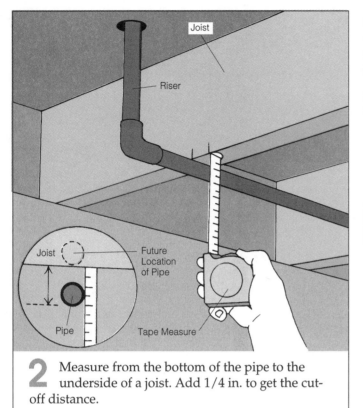

**2** Measure from the bottom of the pipe to the underside of a joist. Add 1/4 in. to get the cut-off distance.

**3** If possible, use a tubing cutter to cut each riser. Then prepare to resolder the pipes and fittings.

copper water pipe is about 1/8 inch larger than its internal dimension, so notches range from about 5/8 inch wide to 1⅛ inches wide.

**2 Measuring for Cuts.** Before removing the pipes figure out how much they have to be raised. To minimize the depth of notches in the joists, the bottom of the pipes can sit flush with the bottom of the joists. Measure from the bottom of a pipe to the underside of a joist. Add 1/4 inch to this dimension to allow for pipe fittings. The total is the amount that needs to be cut off of each riser in order to raise the pipes.

**3 Cutting the Risers.** Use a propane torch to liquefy the solder in the existing fittings so you can disconnect them. Then use a tubing cutter or, if space does not permit, a mini-cutter or a hacksaw to cut the risers. Remove a piece equal in measure to the distance the pipes are to be raised. Then use a handsaw or saber saw to cut notches in the joists. (See page 60.) Use the marks drawn in Step 1 as a guide.

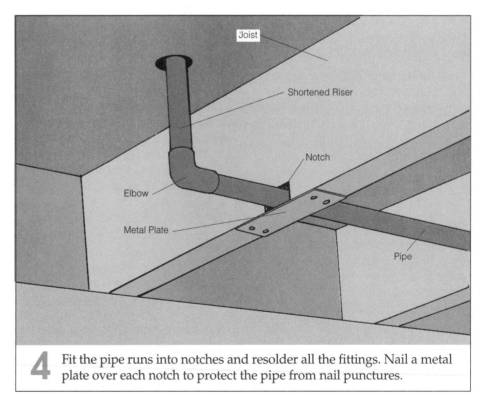

**4** Fit the pipe runs into notches and resolder all the fittings. Nail a metal plate over each notch to protect the pipe from nail punctures.

**4 Reconnecting Pipes.** To promote a good solder joint, clean out the fittings on the existing pipe runs. Then lift the runs into place and solder them together. A metal plate covers each notch to protect piping from possible nail punctures.

# FINISHING WALLS, CEILINGS & FLOORS

After doing all the necessary work to prepare the basement, it is time to install the finished surfaces. These finishing touches determine the character—and comfort— of a basement room.

# Working with Beams & Posts

Beams and posts are part of the structural system that holds a house up and must never be altered, moved or eliminated without the advice of a structural engineer. Unfortunately, posts and beams often are in the way when it comes to remodeling plans.

## Posts

Basement posts typically provide intermediate support for a beam. In most cases, the concrete slab immediately beneath the post has been thickened to form a footing that distributes the structural loads. The top and bottom of each post is toenailed or bolted into place to prevent lateral movement. Posts in older houses usually are made of solid wood, but those used in newer houses are Lally columns. A Lally column essentially is a steel tube that can be adjusted to various heights. It ranges from 3 to 5½ inches in diameter and may be filled with concrete. It sometimes is secured to a wood beam with nails or lag screws that run upward through the top flange.

**Burying Posts.** If a post is not ideally placed in relation to remodeling plans, try to revise the plans rather than deciding immediately to remove the post. The option of moving the post is a last resort. One or more posts may be concealed by "burying" them in a wall that separates two rooms. If the post is unusually wide in diameter, the wall can be framed with 2x6 lumber rather than 2x4 lumber.

If it is not possible to bury the post, it can be disguised. Plywood paneling or drywall can be nailed to a wood post and the edges can be treated just as walls finished with the same materials. Or simply sand the post smooth, round over or chamfer the edges with a router, and paint it.

**Concealing Posts.** If the post is metal, there are several ways to conceal it. One possibility is to apply carpet to it. First test-fit the carpet to make sure it is the right size. Then

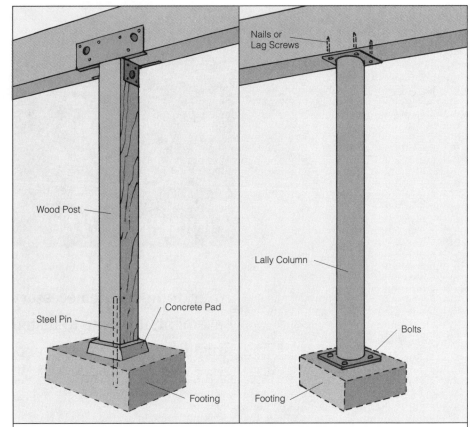

**Posts.** The posts located in the basement rest atop a footing of some type (left). A Lally column is a steel post that ranges from 3 to 5 ½ in. in diameter. It sometimes is secured to a wood beam with nails or lag screws that run upward through the top flange (right).

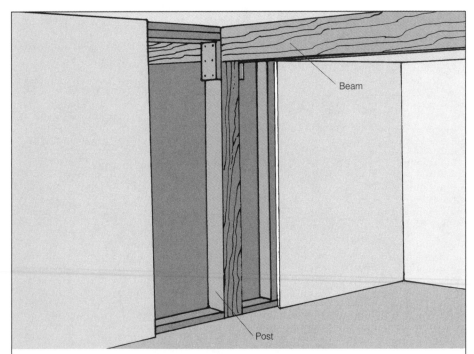

**Burying Posts.** A wood or steel post can be concealed within partition walls. Unusually large posts require a wall framed with 2x6 lumber.

spray or brush both the column and the carpet backing with contact adhesive. When the adhesive becomes tacky, wrap the carpeting around the column. Another option is to build a shelving unit around the post.

## Framing around a Post

One of the best ways to conceal a post or Lally column is to frame around it using lumber. The frame provides a base for other finishes.

**1** **Laying out the Frame.** The outside dimensions of the box can be any dimension as long as the inside dimension is large enough to accommodate the post. It usually is best to minimize the overall size of the box, however, to keep it from overpowering the room. Use a framing square to lay out the inside dimensions of the plates.

**2** **Installing the Frame.** Use 2x3s or 2x4s for the framing lumber. Assemble two opposite walls of the frame to fit between the beam and the floor. Using the layout lines as a position guide, tip the walls into

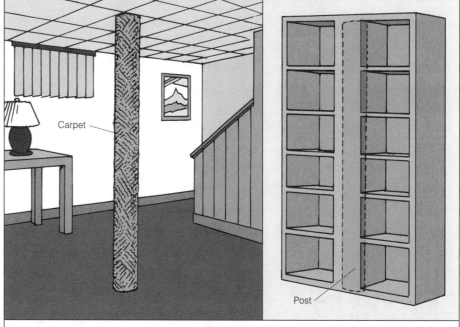

*Concealing Posts.* Carpeting can be applied to the post to conceal it (left). Another option is to build a set of open shelves around the post (right).

place. Then use a level to make sure the frames are plumb. Nail the plates to the floor (using masonry nails if the floor is concrete) and to the underside of the beams above. Cut blocks

to fit between the frames at the top and bottom. Toenail the blocks to the plates. If the frame walls are at all bowed, blocks can be added halfway up the walls to straighten them.

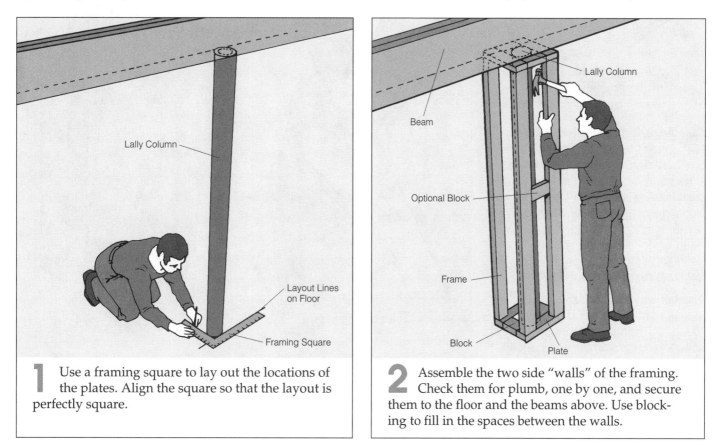

**1** Use a framing square to lay out the locations of the plates. Align the square so that the layout is perfectly square.

**2** Assemble the two side "walls" of the framing. Check them for plumb, one by one, and secure them to the floor and the beams above. Use blocking to fill in the spaces between the walls.

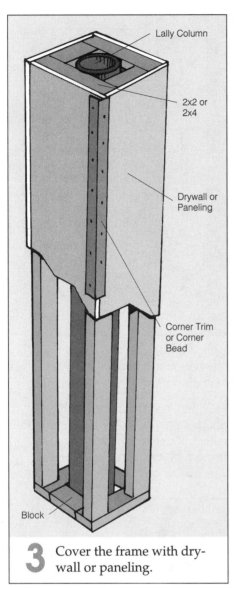

**3** Cover the frame with drywall or paneling.

**3 Applying the Finish Surface.** Once the framing is secure, nail or screw drywall or wood paneling to it the same way it is done for a standard framed wall. Miter the edges of wood paneling or cover them with corner trim. Use standard corner bead when installing drywall.

## Boxing around a Column

Another way to conceal a Lally column is to create a wood box to surround it. This method consumes less space than the frame. (See page 65.) For a concrete floor, glue blocking to the floor to provide nailing. Use 3/4-inch-thick stock to build the box; pine boards or a hardwood such as oak are appropriate. Pine can be painted

or stained, while hardwood can be stained or left natural and then coated with a clear varnish.

**1 Laying out the Box.** Use a framing square to lay out the inside perimeter of the box. The outside perimeter then can be drawn 3/4 inch outside of the first line, providing the exact outside dimensions of the sides of the box.

**2 Cutting the Sides.** Measure the distance between floor and ceiling and subtract 1/4 inch from this measurement to provide a fitting allowance. Cut four pieces of stock to length. Use a table saw to miter each edge. Then test-fit the assembly around the post.

**3 Assembling and Installing the Box.** Spread a thin film of wood glue on the edges and use finishing nails to nail three sides of the box together. Then slip the three sides over the post and nail the fourth side into place. Toenail the box into the floor as well as the beam above.

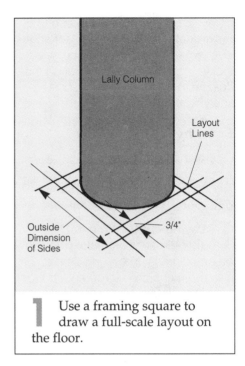

**1** Use a framing square to draw a full-scale layout on the floor.

**2** Use a table saw or circular saw to miter the sides. For safety, use a blade guard (not shown here for clarity) on the table saw.

**3** Glue and nail three sides together, and then slip the assembly over the post and nail on the fourth side. Toenail the box to the floor and the beam.

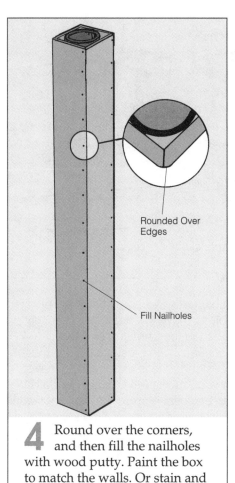

Rounded Over
Edges

Fill Nailholes

**4** Round over the corners, and then fill the nailholes with wood putty. Paint the box to match the walls. Or stain and then use putty.

**4** **Finishing the Box.** Use sandpaper or a rasp to round over the edges of the box. Typically, a post is located in the middle of a room and sanding it minimizes impact damage, both to the box and

to those who may bump into it accidentally. Sand it smooth, stain it, and then fill the holes with putty. The box can also be painted.

## Types of Beams

A beam provides intermediate support for floor joists. Like posts, beams cannot be removed or relocated with ease. Luckily, however, they do not obstruct floor plans as much as posts do. Remember, though, that building codes call for at least 84 inches of headroom beneath a beam.

In newer homes, steel or glue-laminated wood typically is used for beams that span more than 8 feet. A solid-wood beam is sufficient for smaller spans. Flitch beams, made up of a sandwich of wood and metal, combine the strength of steel with the look and lighter weight of wood.

**Beam Connections.** The connection between a post and a beam must be rigid. Depending on the type of post and the type of column, there are several ways to achieve a rigid connection. A metal saddle sometimes is installed around the beam. This type of saddle has flanges that are nailed to wooden posts. Another type of saddle goes around the beam and is welded to a metal post. Two beams that meet over a single post must be connected to one another as well as to the post. This usually is done with a metal strap.

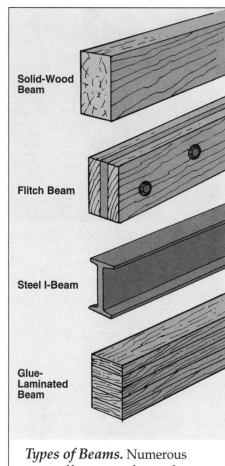

Solid-Wood
Beam

Flitch Beam

Steel I-Beam

Glue-
Laminated
Beam

*Types of Beams.* Numerous types of beams can be used to support joists in a basement. Shown here are the most common.

If drywall or paneling is to be applied to the beam, these connections may get in the way. However, never remove a connection without replacing it with something of equal strength.

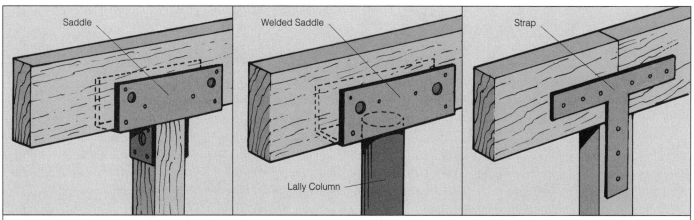

Saddle

Welded Saddle

Lally Column

Strap

*Beam Connections.* There are several ways to secure a beam to a post. Although these connections sometimes get in the way when drywall is being installed, they must never be removed without replacing them with something equally strong. Use screws, nails, or lag bolts to complete the connection.

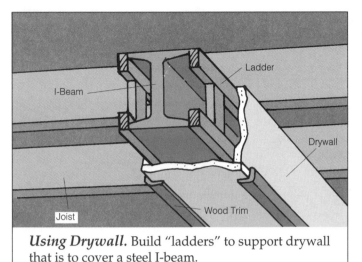

*Using Drywall.* Build "ladders" to support drywall that is to cover a steel I-beam.

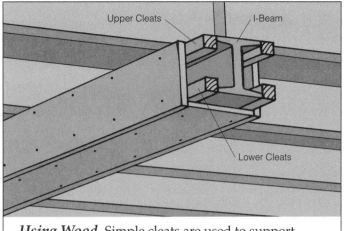

*Using Wood.* Simple cleats are used to support wood around a steel I-beam.

## Concealing a Beam

The task of concealing a wood beam, like the task of concealing a post, is not difficult. A steel beam, on the other hand, is not easy to conceal. (It is never easy to drill into a steel beam.) To get around this problem, paneling or drywall is secured to a wood framework that is nailed to the underside of the ceiling joists.

**Using Drywall.** First, build two wood ladders made of 1x3s. Place the ladders against the beam and then toe-nail them to the joists. Attach drywall on all three sides. Before finishing the walls, cover the drywall joints with drywall corner bead or wood trim.

**Using Wood.** To make the job of covering the beam easier, use 3/8-inch or thicker paneling, plywood or solid wood. Attach cleats to the joists against both sides of the beam. Then use glue and finishing nails to attach cleats along one inside edge of the wood side panels. (Nail through the panels into the cleats.) Glue and nail the side panels to the upper cleats. Then glue and nail the bottom panel to the lower cleats.

## Concealing Ducts

A large, rectangular sheet metal duct (called a trunk) often leads from the furnace to the farthest points of the basement. Smaller ducts branch away from the trunk and distribute air to each room above. The ducts in a central air-conditioning system may have a similar layout. If the ducts

obstruct headroom, it may be possible to move them but this definitely is a job for a heating or cooling contractor. In most cases, it is much easier and less expensive to leave the ducts in place. It may be possible to enclose them within the confines of a suspended ceiling. If a suspended ceiling is not feasible, however, the ducts can be boxed within a wood and paneling framework.

## Concealing Soil Pipes

The soil pipe (the main drain line of a house) conducts water and waste away from the house. Typically, it is the largest pipe in the basement and may be plastic or cast iron. If possible, enclose the pipe within a box or a soffit. It is a good idea to wrap the

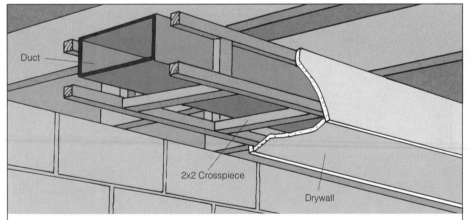

*Concealing Ducts.* Heating and air-conditioning ducts are concealed as if they were beams. Ducts that run alongside beams can be enclosed in the same box.

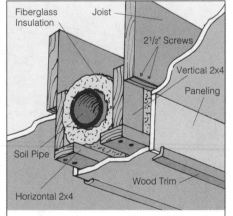

*Concealing Soil Pipes.* A soil pipe can be boxed-in as if it were a steel beam or a heating duct.

pipe in insulation before it is boxed, especially if it is plastic. The insulation reduces the sound of rushing water. Be sure to take measurements in several places along the length of the pipe, however, because it must slope at least 1/4 inch per foot in order to drain properly. If the soil pipe's cleanout plug is covered up, include a door for access to the plug.

# Painting Masonry Walls

Great lengths can be taken in trying to make a basement seem less like a basement, but maybe your goal simply is to brighten up the place without devoting so much time to the project. If maximum impact and minimum expense and effort are what you are after, consider painting the walls. Poured concrete and concrete block walls can be painted successfully, but the paint cannot cover defects. Cracks, flaws, and mortar joints show just as clearly after painting as before. In fact, they may stand out even more when the walls become a consistent color.

For paint to adhere properly, it must be applied to a surface that is free of dirt, dust, and grease. In a basement, it is especially important that the surface is dry. If the wall is susceptible to moisture problems, the problems must be corrected first or the paint will flake off the wall. (See page 20.) The care that is invested in cleaning, scraping, and patching the walls makes the effort of painting worthwhile.

## *Types of Paints*

Standard latex paints are water-based, easy to clean up, and quick to dry. Instead of water, oil-based paints use natural or synthetic oil as the vehicle for carrying the pigments. They take longer to dry and require solvents for thinning paint and cleaning tools. They also call for plenty of ventilation to dispel fumes. Basements are not easy to ventilate, so it is better to use latex paint. No matter

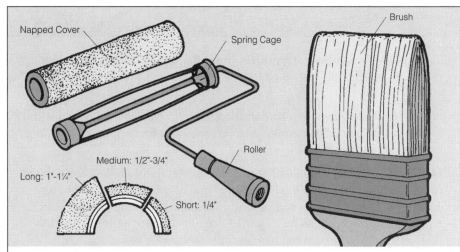

***Brushes and Rollers.*** Masonry surfaces, particularly concrete block, are fairly rough. To paint these surfaces quickly use a roller frame and a long-napped roller cover. A brush is needed for touching up corners and edges.

what kind of paint is used, the masonry surfaces have to be cleaned and primed before painting can begin. (Various priming products are available.)

Though not quite a paint, another colored surface coating can be applied to basement walls, particularly if minor moisture problems are evident. Called "masonry waterproofer," it is a ready-mixed coating that contains synthetic rubber and portland cement. (Some formulations are latex-based to reduce fumes.) The product comes in several standard colors and can be tinted lightly to produce other colors. Two coats of this product actually seal the surface from minor moisture penetration, even if that moisture is driven by hydrostatic pressure. Masonry waterproofers are applied with a brush, not a roller, to ensure that the pores of the masonry are sealed adequately. There is no need to paint over waterproofer that is tinted, although you can paint over it with a latex paint. (See page 21.)

**Brushes and Rollers.** Basement walls can be painted entirely with a brush, but a roller completes the job faster. A roller consists of a frame and a cover. Covers vary in thickness and nap composition. A short nap, about 1/4 inch thick, applies a thin,

smooth layer of paint and is suitable for the smooth surface of a poured-concrete wall. A longer nap, about 1 inch thick, deposits a large amount of paint and is better for porous or irregular surfaces such as concrete block. Other necessary items include a roller pan for loading the roller with paint and a 3- or 4-inch paintbrush for painting into corners and around details. A natural-bristle brush is best for oil-based paint; use synthetic-bristle brushes for latex paint. (The water in latex paint ruins natural bristles.)

# Drywall

Drywall (also known as plasterboard, gypsum board, or wallboard or by the trade name Sheetrock) is a popular option for finishing walls. It is readily available, relatively easy to work with, and inexpensive.

## *Types of Drywall*

Regular drywall has a dark gray kraft-paper backing. The front is covered with smooth, off-white paper that takes paint readily. The long edges of each sheet are tapered slightly to accept tape and joint compound. Standard drywall comes in several thicknesses; 1/2 inch is suitable for basements. Some types of drywall have special purposes.

## Tips for Nailing Drywall

To install 1/2-inch-thick drywall use nails that are 1⅜ inches long. Use only nails specifically designed for use with drywall.

Space nails 7 inches apart on ceilings and 8 inches apart on walls. Do not nail closer than 3/8 inch or further than 1/2 inch from the edge of a sheet. Sheets can be placed horizontally or vertically but there must be a nailing surface behind every seam.

***Drywall Hammer.*** The head of each nail is set slightly below the surface of the drywall. This is called "dimpling" and allows the nailhead to be concealed later with joint compound. A standard hammer cannot form a proper dimple because it is likely to damage the face paper of the drywall. If the nail is driven too hard and the face paper is damaged, the nail will not hold well. To ensure proper holding, drive a second nail nearby. Use a special drywall hammer, which has a slightly concave face, instead. Rather than claws, this hammer has a flat edge that can be used to pry drywall into tight spots. A similar tool with a sharpened edge is called a drywall hatchet.

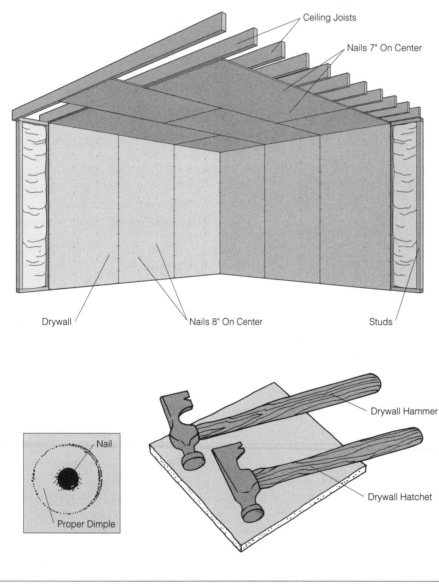

Ceiling Joists

Nails 7" On Center

Drywall

Nails 8" On Center

Studs

Nail

Proper Dimple

Drywall Hammer

Drywall Hatchet

Water-resistant drywall, usually blue or green in color, is made for use in areas of high moisture, such as around bathtubs. Fire-resistant drywall, called Type X, sometimes is required by building codes in certain areas, such as around a furnace enclosure.

### Estimating Drywall

Calculate the square footage of the ceiling and each wall, then add these figures to get a total for the

### Nails vs Screws

Nails suffice for small drywall jobs and patches. Use 1⅜-inch ring-shank drywall nails for 1/2-inch wallboard, and 1½-inch nails for 5/8-inch material. For larger jobs, such as an entire room, consider using drywall screws that are at least 3/4-inch longer than the thickness of the wallboard.

**Drywall Screwdriver.** A variable-speed electric drill fitted with a Phillips-head bit or a drywall screwdriver (an electric drill with a special head) is used to drive drywall screws. The latter can be rented from a tool rental store. These "screw guns" come with a clutch that sinks the screw just below the surface of the drywall without breaking the paper surface. These small dimples are easy to fill with joint compound.

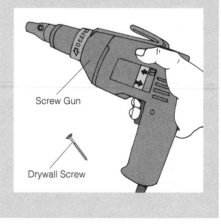

Screw Gun

Drywall Screw

entire room. Add about 10 percent to this (to account for waste) and divide by 32 (the number of square feet in one 4x8-foot sheet). The result is the approximate number of 4x8-foot drywall panels needed for the job. If the room has complicated or odd-shaped surfaces, a more detailed estimate can be done. Draw each surface to scale, and then determine the most efficient layout of panels.

## Installing Drywall

**1** **Cutting Drywall.** Plan your cuts so that end joints on walls and ceilings will be staggered. This will look better when finished than continuous joints, and makes for stronger construction. Place one sheet on a flat work surface and use a utility knife guided by a straightedge to score the face paper. Shift the drywall so the score line overhangs the work surface, and snap it along the line. Then slice through the paper backing to remove the piece. When using a utility knife, keep your fingers well away from the cut line.

**2** **Installing Drywall on the Ceiling.** A 4x8-foot sheet of drywall is heavy and awkward to handle, so get some assistance. Cut a sheet to size (if necessary), and then lift it into place and hold it firmly

**1** Score a straight line on the face of a drywall sheet, and then snap it along that line.

against the joists. To hold the sheet in place, nail several nails into its center. With a helper or two still supporting the sheet, use a chalkline to mark the position of joists and complete the nailing. (A simple T-brace can also be used to support the drywall temporarily.)

**3** **Installing Drywall on Walls.** Install the drywall vertically so that the tapered edges of each sheet fall over a stud (or over a wood cleat). If the panel has to be lifted slightly to maneuver it into position,

use scraps of wood to make a foot-operated lifting lever. The top edge of the wall panel butts against the ceiling panel that is already in place. If the concrete floors remain exposed, lift the drywall about 1/2 inch above the floor before nailing it. This prevents the drywall from absorbing moisture from the concrete.

**4** **Marking for Cutouts.** To accommodate electrical boxes, cut holes in the drywall. Measure the location of the box, and transfer the measurements to the drywall. Or

**2** Press the sheet against the ceiling joists and nail from the center of the panel towards the edges.

**3** Use a lever to help lift drywall sheets into place. Another approach is to rest the sheet on a small scrap of wood.

**4** Mark obstructions, such as an electrical box, with lipstick and press the drywall against it. This transfers a layout mark to the back of the panel.

mark the outside edges of each box with lipstick, and then cut a sheet of drywall to the proper size and push it firmly into position. (The print of lipstick indicates where to make the hole.) Use a keyhole saw or drywall saw to cut the hole.

## Finishing Drywall

After the drywall is in place, all of the seams and nail dimples (as well as imperfections such as accidental gouges) are concealed in a multi-step process called "finishing." Even the smallest dents and ridges show through paint and wallpaper, so this work must be done meticulously.

### Tools & Materials

A thick, paste-like material called joint compound is the main ingredient for finishing drywall. Several layers of compound are spread over seams and imperfections and each layer is sanded smooth if necessary after it dries. Compound comes in several formulas but "all-purpose compound" is suitable for most applications. Inexpensive paper tape, which is sold by the roll, is embedded in the compound to reinforce seams. It prevents cracks from appearing at these locations. A 100-grit sandpaper is used to smooth dried joint compound. Any type can be used but silicon-carbide paper does not wear out as quickly as standard papers. Even better, if available, is drywall sanding mesh. It lasts a long time and does not become clogged with drywall dust.

Several taping knives of different sizes are used to spread the compound and smooth wet seams. Each knife has a thin, spring-steel blade. Though knife size is partly a matter of personal preference, a 4- to 6-inch knife works well for the first coat and for filling nail dimples. On the other hand, 10- and 14-inch knives are good for smoothing joints.

**1** **Filling Flat Joints.** Use the smallest knife to apply compound to a joint. Force enough compound into the tapered drywall joints to level

them. At butt joints (where the non-tapered ends of two panels join) fill the crack, creating a slight hump. (This hump is flattened later.)

**2** **Embedding the Tape.** Cut a length of joint tape and center one end of it over the joint, then embed the tape by using the 4-inch knife to smooth it into the compound. Spread a layer of compound about 1/8 inch thick over the tape while holding the knife at a 45-degree angle. Then go over the joint again to scrape away the excess compound.

**3** **Finishing Inside Corners.** Start by spreading a 2- or 3-inch

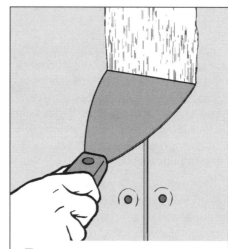

**1** Use the smallest knife to apply joint compound to a seam. The compound fills the tapered area between two drywall sheets.

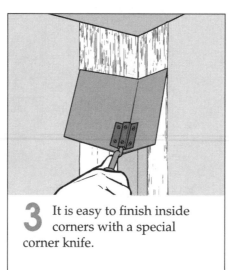

**3** It is easy to finish inside corners with a special corner knife.

swath of compound on both sides of the inside corner joints. Fold a length of paper tape along its centerline and apply it to the joint. (The tape is precreased for this purpose.) Remove excess compound. (See Step 2.) An angled taping knife (called an inside corner taping tool) makes this task easier.

**4** **Finishing Outside Corners.** When working with outside corners, use tin snips to cut a length of metal corner bead to the height of the wall. Angle the cut ends inward slightly to ensure a better fit. Use drywall nails to nail the bead to the

**2** Cut paper reinforcing tape to the length of the seam, then center it over the seam and use the smallest knife to smooth it into place.

**4** The knife rides along the edge of the corner bead as the compound is spread. Make sure nails are set below this level.

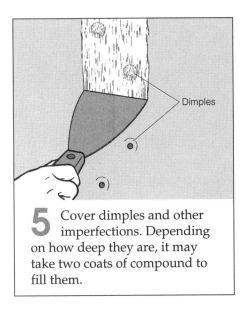

**5** Cover dimples and other imperfections. Depending on how deep they are, it may take two coats of compound to fill them.

**6** Joints are covered with three layers of compound spread in successively wider swaths. The top layer requires a light sanding.

**7** When the compound is completely dry, sand all joints and dimples smooth.

wall. The nails must be set below the level of the edge of the bead. To make sure they are, run a dry knife over the bead before the compound is spread. If the nails are too high, the blade will hit them. After all the nails are set, use the edge of the bead to guide the knife as it fills the corner bead with joint compound.

**5** **Filling Nail Dimples.** Use the smallest knife to fill nail dimples and other minor imperfections with compound. No tape is required.

**6** **Applying Finish Coats.** After the first coat is dry inspect the seams and smooth out ridges that might interfere with the smoothness of subsequent joints: Use the 4-inch knife to scrape off the ridges or lightly sand them. (With practice the first coat will be smooth enough that this step can be skipped.) Then use the 10-inch knife to apply a thin second coat of compound to the joints. Use the small knife to "spot" the dimples again. After the second coat dries, use the 14-inch knife to spread the third and final coat. Spot dimples only if they are not filled completely.

**7** **Sanding the Compound.** After 24 hours, or when it is completely dry, sand all joints and dimples smooth. Shine a bright floodlight across the walls to detect ridges and improperly filled nail dimples. (Under the light imperfections become immediately apparent.) Fold a sheet

of 100-grit sandpaper in quarters and go over the compound lightly. Do not sand through the drywall's paper facing. To make the work easier use a universal pole sander. This tool has a pad with clamps to hold sandpaper or drywall mesh. The pad is swivel-mounted to a pole. A pole sander particularly is handy for reaching ceilings, but it can be used almost everywhere because it extends your sanding stroke. Sanding dust is very fine, so use goggles and a dust mask (or respirator) when sanding. Brush or vacuum all traces of dust before painting or papering the walls.

## Suspended Ceilings

Deciding what kind of ceiling to install in a new basement room is not just a matter of appearance. More importantly, it is a matter of how much headroom there is and how many ducts, pipes and wires crisscross the underside of the joists. Often the best way to solve the latter issue is to install a suspended ceiling system (if a lack of headroom does not prevent it).

A suspended ceiling (sometimes called a dropped or exposed grid ceiling) is a gridlike framework of metal channels that hangs beneath the joists on short lengths of wire. The metal channels support lightweight acoustical panels that form the finished surface of the ceiling. The

beauty of this system is that it conceals obstructions attached to the underside of the joists yet allows easy access for fixing pipes or adding wiring later on. Another advantage is that the ceiling is leveled as it is installed; the existing joists need not be level or even straight. A suspended ceiling system also makes the job of installing ceiling lights easier: Simply remove an acoustical tile and replace it with a special drop-in fluorescent fixture.

### *Parts of a Suspended Ceiling*

There are five key parts of a suspended ceiling system. Main runners are the primary support members and are arranged in parallel rows that run the length of the room. Main runners come in a variety of finishes and in several shapes. Cross runners are lighter-gauge supports that fit between the main runners at right angles. Hangers are lengths of lightweight (usually 18-gauge) wire. One end is hooked into holes in the main runners while the other end is attached to the joists. Acoustical ceiling panels fit into the grid that is created by the runners. They can be square or rectangular and come in a variety of sizes and patterns. Wall molding is a metal channel that is attached to the walls. It supports ceiling panels around the perimeter of the room.

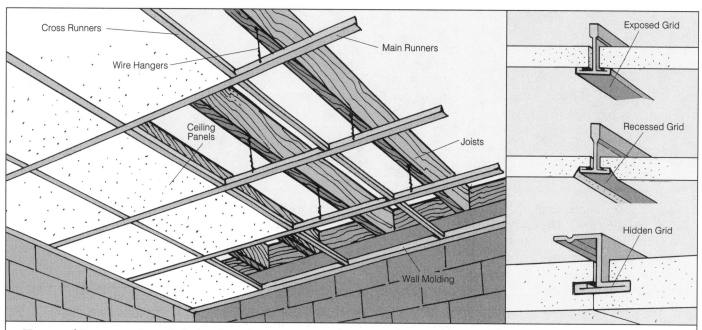

**Types of Runners.** Suspended ceilings are comprised of the parts shown here. Runners are the primary support system for the ceiling. The look of the ceiling changes according to the type of runners used.

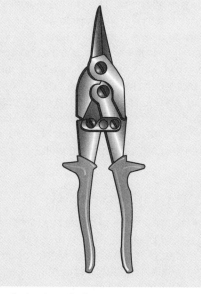

**Aviation Snips.** The leverage provided by the hinged jaws of the snips makes it easy to cut metal ceiling runners.

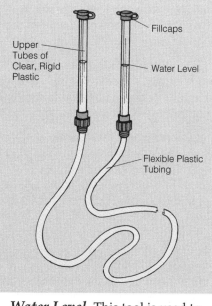

**Water Level.** This tool is used to locate points around the room that are exactly at the same level.

**Types of Runners.** There are three styles of runners, each of which gives the ceiling a different look. The runners can be completely exposed beneath the panels, they can be recessed into lips on the panel edges or they can be hidden in slots in the panel edges.

## Tools

Many of the tools needed for this project are basic: a hammer, chalkline, combination square, levels, a hacksaw, plumb bob, and a utility knife. The following describes a few special tools needed for the job:

**Aviation Snips.** This tool easily cuts the light-gauge metals used to support acoustical ceilings. The snips are designed for maximum leverage on the workpiece. They have a spring action that opens the tool after a cut. Snips are available in right-hand, left-hand, and straight-cut models.

**Water Level.** The premise behind this tool is simple: Water always seeks its own level. Thus, water contained in clear plastic tubing can be used to locate points around the room that are exactly at the same level. Though professional ceiling installers use a laser level to do the same thing, a simple water level is inexpensive and foolproof, and it can be purchased at hardware and home center stores.

## Installing a Suspended Ceiling

**1** **Planning the Job.** Panels are available in 2x2-foot and 2x4-foot sizes. The latter works best if fluorescent lighting is to be placed in the ceiling because it fits the standard fluorescent tube length. Smaller panels require more cross runners so the job is more time-consuming. Wall molding and main runners are sold in different lengths up to 12 feet and can be overlapped to reach greater distances. Cross runners are 24 inches long. To help estimate the amount of materials needed for the job, draw a plan view of the ceiling.

**2** **Establishing Benchmarks.** The key to success is making sure the ceiling is level across the entire room. Existing floor and ceiling surfaces may not be level so never use them as reference points for measuring. Instead, establish benchmarks on the walls at every corner. (Use a water level to ensure that every benchmark is precisely located.) Benchmarks can be placed at any height, but 60 inches is most convenient. Future measurements are taken from these benchmarks.

**3** **Determining Ceiling Height.** The standard ceiling height is 90 inches; it also is the minimum height for lighting in a suspended ceiling. The ceiling must not be closer than 3 inches to projections. Hang it completely below projections or use drywall or wood paneling to box-in the projections. (See page 68.) Once the ceiling height has been determined, measure up from the benchmarks to locate the position of

the wall molding. Snap a chalkline on the walls around the perimeter of the room. It is best to draw this line in the place where the top edge of the molding is to be located; the chalk marks will not be visible after the ceiling molding is in place.

**4** **Installing Wall Molding.** Nail molding to the walls, making sure each nail penetrates a stud. Use the aviation snips to miter the molding at inside and outside corners. When cutting wall molding to length remember to account for the thickness of the adjacent wall molding. Butt lengths of wall molding where they meet midwall.

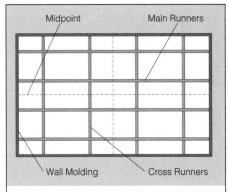

**1** Use the plan view to determine the number of cross runners and ceiling panels needed as well as the lineal footage of the main runners.

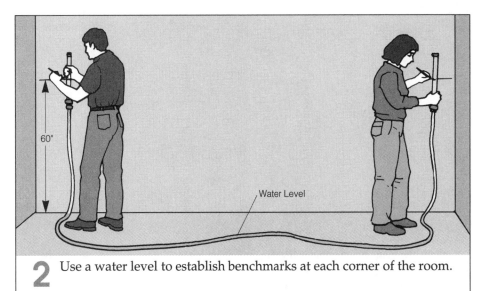

**2** Use a water level to establish benchmarks at each corner of the room.

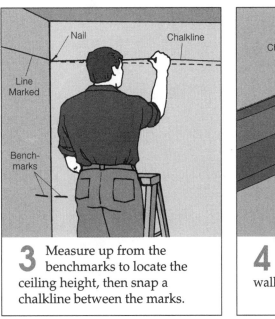

**3** Measure up from the benchmarks to locate the ceiling height, then snap a chalkline between the marks.

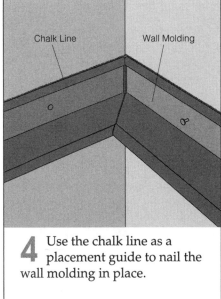

**4** Use the chalk line as a placement guide to nail the wall molding in place.

**5 Establishing Centerlines.** Measure the length and width of the room, and divide these measurements in half to get the centerpoint of each wall. Use layout strings to connect opposing midpoints, stretching them tightly between the wall molding. Check the intersection of the two strings to make sure they are square to each other. If not, adjust one or the other slightly until they are square. It is easier to adjust layout strings when they are attached to nails that can be wedged behind the wall molding.

**6 Adjusting the Layout.** Plan the layout of ceiling panels to minimize the need for small pieces around the border of the ceiling. Doing so creates a better-looking job. If the border tiles will be less than half the width of a field tile, adjust the layout one way or the other to eliminate this unsightly condition.

**7 Installing Guidelines.** Plan to install the first main runner approximately parallel to the wall and at a distance from the wall that is equal to the width of the border units. Make measurements from the centerlines rather than from the wall itself. (The wall might not be square.) Stretch a guideline between the wall moldings at these points.

**8 Attaching Hanger Wires.** Start with the joists at either end of the ceiling. Install an eyescrew (or fastener supplied by the ceiling manufacturer) into every fourth joist directly above the guideline. Twist a piece of hanger wire through each eyescrew so that it hangs about 6 inches below the guideline. Cut a main runner to length, and hang it from the wires so that it is just barely above the guideline. Twist the wires to secure the runner in position.

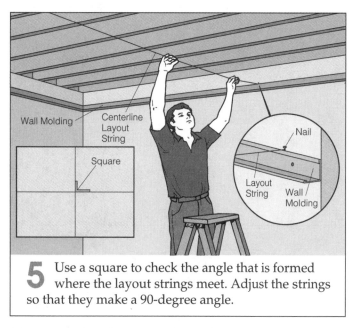

**5** Use a square to check the angle that is formed where the layout strings meet. Adjust the strings so that they make a 90-degree angle.

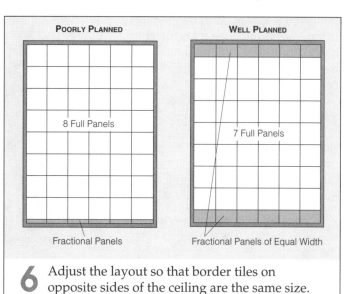

**6** Adjust the layout so that border tiles on opposite sides of the ceiling are the same size.

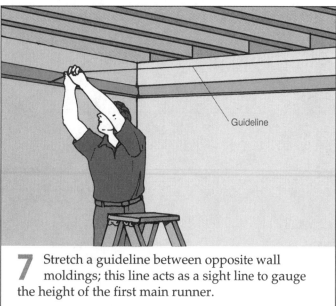

**7** Stretch a guideline between opposite wall moldings; this line acts as a sight line to gauge the height of the first main runner.

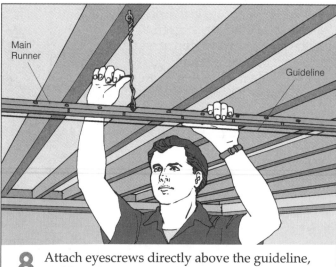

**8** Attach eyescrews directly above the guideline, and loop hanger wire through each eyescrew. Secure the main runner to the wire.

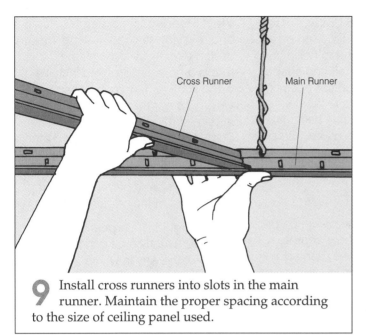

Cross Runner    Main Runner

**9** Install cross runners into slots in the main runner. Maintain the proper spacing according to the size of ceiling panel used.

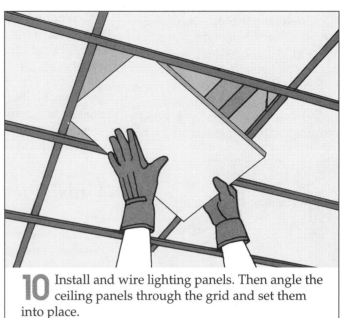

**10** Install and wire lighting panels. Then angle the ceiling panels through the grid and set them into place.

**9** **Installing Cross Runners.** Slip the first cross runner in between the main runner and the wall molding. (It locks into the main runner's prepunched holes.) Install the next main runner by using cross runners to gauge its spacing. Continue to work across the room until all of the runners have been installed.

**10** **Placing Ceiling Panels.** Lift each ceiling panel into place by turning it at an angle and pushing it into the grid of runners. Use a utility knife and a straightedge to cut panels at the borders as needed. When handling panels, wear clean, lightweight gloves so the finished surfaces do not become smudged.

## Working around Obstructions

**1** **Hanging Runners below the Obstruction.** If a pipe or duct intrudes below the level of the ceiling, it can be boxed in with pieces of the grid system. U-shaped channel molding and extra wall molding is needed for this job. Include the box in original layout plans and leave the ceiling open for now. Use the aviation snips to cut 90-degree notches in lengths of main runner, then bend the runners at these points to form the "ribs" of the box.

**2** **Attaching U-Channel.** Fasten U-channel to the ceiling grid along the length of the obstruction. Then use pop rivets to attach the ribs to the U-channel. (A pop rivet gun is an inexpensive tool available at hardware stores).

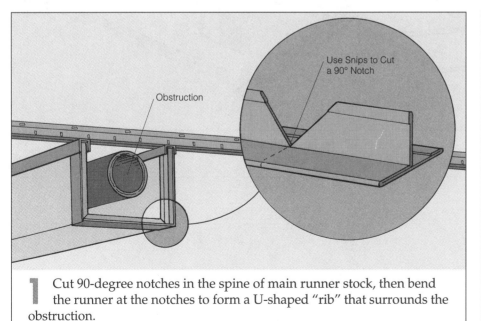

Obstruction

Use Snips to Cut a 90° Notch

**1** Cut 90-degree notches in the spine of main runner stock, then bend the runner at the notches to form a U-shaped "rib" that surrounds the obstruction.

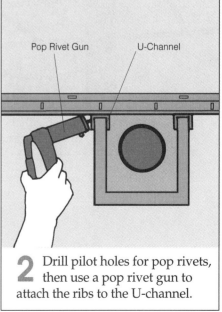

Pop Rivet Gun    U-Channel

**2** Drill pilot holes for pop rivets, then use a pop rivet gun to attach the ribs to the U-channel.

**3** **Installing the Panels.** Connect the ribs with lengths of wall molding and cut ceiling panels to fit the box as needed. Install the vertical panels first; they are locked in place when the horizontal panels are installed. Use hanger wire as needed to provide additional support for the box.

**4** **Working around Posts.** There are two ways to deal with posts that penetrate suspended ceilings. Either cut a panel in half and shape the pieces to fit around the post, or use additional runners to box in the post. If the panel is cut in half, the seam between halves usually is self-supporting and unobtrusive.

## Finish Flooring

Once the subfloor is in place, carpeting and sheet-vinyl floors can be installed in the usual way. An additional layer of plywood underlayment usually is required beneath sheet vinyl, but carpeting and a carpet pad can be installed directly over the subfloor.

Hardwood flooring can be installed over concrete, but it is not recommended for use over a below-grade basement slab because of potential moisture problems. If the slab is unusually dry, however, consult a flooring specialist to see if an exception can be made.

**Vinyl Flooring.** If the slab is smooth and dry, vinyl flooring may be installed directly over the slab. If moisture is a potential problem install a wood subfloor before installing sheet vinyl. This approach also makes for a more comfortable, resilient floor. Some flooring products require that the vinyl be imbedded entirely in mastic. Others, however, require only a perimeter band of mastic to hold the flooring at the edges of the room.

**Carpeting.** Most carpets cannot be installed directly over concrete because of the way in which they are stretched between tack-strips. Many nails are used to secure the tack strips (an unrealistic proposition if the substrate is concrete). Cushion-backed carpet may be installed directly on the slab but before doing so discuss this possibility with the manufacturer—some manufacturers do not recommend this type of installation because of potential mildew problems. Cushion-backed carpeting is not recommended for use on stairs.

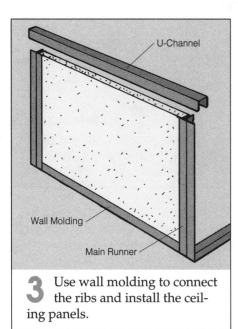

**3** Use wall molding to connect the ribs and install the ceiling panels.

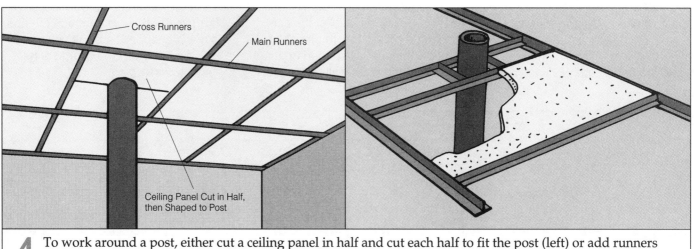

**4** To work around a post, either cut a ceiling panel in half and cut each half to fit the post (left) or add runners and small pieces of ceiling panel to enclose it (right).

**Actual Dimension** The exact measurements of a piece of lumber after it has been cut, surfaced, and dried. Example: A 2x4's actual dimensions are 1½x 3½ inches.

**Building Codes** Municipal rules regulating safe building practices and procedures. Generally, the codes encompass structural, electrical, plumbing, and mechanical remodeling and new construction. Confirmation of conformity to local codes by inspection may be required.

**Butt Joint** A joint in which a square-cut piece of wood is attached to the end or face of a second piece.

**Cable Staples** Heavy-duty staples driven into framing and used to support cable when running wire.

**Circuit Breaker** A protective device that opens a circuit, cutting off the power automatically when a given overcurrent occurs. Can also be operated and reset manually.

**Conduit** Metal or plastic tubing designed to enclose electrical wires.

**Drywall** Also known as wallboard, gypsum board, plasterboard, and by the trade name Sheetrock; a paper-covered sandwich of gypsum plaster used for wall and ceiling surfacing.

**DWV (Drain, waste, vent system)** The system of piping and fittings inside the walls used to carry away plumbing drainage and waste.

**Ground-Fault Circuit Interrupter (GFCI)** A safety circuit breaker that compares the amount of current entering a receptacle on the hot wire with the amount leaving on the white wire. If there is a discrepancy of 0.005 volt, the GFCI breaks the circuit in a fraction of a second. The device is usually required by code in areas subject to dampness such as bathrooms, kitchens, and outdoor areas.

**Header** A structural member that forms the top of a window, door, skylight, or other opening to provide framing support and transfer weight loads. Header thickness should equal wall width.

**Inspection** Whenever a permit is required, it is necessary to schedule a time for a city or county building inspector to visit your home and examine the work.

**Jamb** The inside face of a window or door; liner.

**Joist** One in a series of parallel framing members that supports a floor or ceiling load. Joists are supported by beams, girders, or bearing walls.

**Load-bearing Wall** A wall that is used to support the house structure and transfer weight to the foundation.

**Miter** A joint in which the ends of two pieces of wood are cut at equal angles (typically 45 degrees) to form a corner.

**National Electrical Code** Body of regulations spelling out safe, functional electrical procedures. Local codes can add to but not delete from NEC regulations.

**Nominal Dimension** The identifying dimensions of a piece of lumber (e.g., 2x4) which are larger than the actual dimensions (1½ x 3½).

**On Center** A point of reference for measuring. For example, "16 inches on center" means 16 inches from the center of one framing member to the center of the next.

**Partition Wall** A wall that divides space. It may be load-bearing or nonload-bearing.

**Penny (abbreviated "d")** Unit of nail measurement. Example: A 10d nail is 3 inches long.

**Permit** A license that authorizes local municipality permission to do work on your home. Minor repairs and remodeling work usually do not call for a permit, but if the job consists of extending the water supply and the drain, waste, vent system, adding an electrical circuit, or making structural changes to a building, a permit may be necessary.

**Polyethylene Sheet** A plastic material well suited to retard vapor passage in a floor, wall, or ceiling. Common thicknesses are 4, 6, and 8 mils.

**Post** A vertical support member. In a basement, the post typically provides intermediate support for a beam or girder. In most cases, the concrete slab immediately beneath the post has been thickened to form a footing that distributes the structural loads.

**R-value** A number assigned to thermal insulation to measure the insulation's resistance to heat flow. The higher the number, the better the insulation.

**Radon** A colorless, odorless radioactive gas that comes from the natural breakdown of uranium in soil, rock, and water. When inhaled, molecules of radon lodge in the lungs and may lead to an increased risk of lung cancer.

**Rigid Insulation** Boards of insulation that are composed of various types of plastics. Rigid insulation offers the highest R-value per inch.

**Romex** A brand name for plastic-sheathed cable containing at least two conductors.

**Service Entrance Panel** The point at which electricity provided by a local utility enters a house wiring system.

**Sistering** The process of reinforcing a framing member by joining another piece of lumber alongside it.

**Sleepers** Boards laid over a concrete floor as a foundation for the subflooring of a new floor.

**Soil Pipe** The main drain line of a house, it conducts water and waste away from the house. Typically, it is the largest pipe in the basement and may be plastic or cast iron.

**Stud** Vertical member of a frame wall, placed at both ends and most often every 16 inches on center. Provides structural framing and facilitates covering with drywall or plywood.

**Subfloor** The floor surface below a finished floor. Usually made of sheet material such as plywood; in older houses it is likely to consist of diagonally attached boards.

**Sump Pump** A device that draws unwanted water from beneath the slab and pumps it away from the house.

**Toenail** Joining two boards together by nailing at an angle through the end, or toe, on one board and into the face of another.

**Top Plate** Horizontal framing member, usually a 2x4, that sits on the top of wall studs and supports floor joists and rafters.

**Underwriters Laboratories (UL)** Independent organization that tests electrical products for safe operation and conformance with published standards under various conditions. Products that pass may display the UL logo.

**Vapor Barrier** Material—usually plastic—used to block out the flow of moisture.

**Window Well** Made of concrete blocks or galvanized steel, a window well holds soil away from a window that is located partially below grade.